BACH'S 'BRANDENBURG' CONCERTOS

BACH'S
BRANDENBURG
CONCERTOS

BY

NORMAN CARRELL

Foreword by
Yehudi Menuhin

London
GEORGE ALLEN & UNWIN LTD
RUSKIN HOUSE MUSEUM STREET

FIRST PUBLISHED IN 1963

PRINTED IN GREAT BRITAIN
AND SET IN 10 ON 11 PT. SPECTRUM
BY NOVELLO AND COMPANY LIMITED
AND BOUND BY KEY AND WHITING LIMITED
LONDON

FOREWORD

If my own experience can serve as an example, then I can say without reservation that Mr. Norman Carrell will bring to all his readers that sense of real enjoyment, so peculiarly English, that comes of scholarship which, however profound, is both undogmatic and adventurous.

Many are the pleasant hours we spent together some years ago discussing this fascinating subject in its historical, musical and human aspect—hours which helped to round out my understanding of the fascinating and informal masterpieces and hours which, I like to think, may have provided the first prompting to Mr. Norman Carrell to collect the fruit of his scholarship and imagination in book form. I am sure he has succeeded in retaining in the pages following the same spontaneity and charm that marked our conversations.

YEHUDI MENUHIN
August, 1963

INTRODUCTION

This book discusses the historical background of the concertos, the orchestras for which they may have been written, the instruments employed and certain points of interest in their performance. Also it contains a short analysis of the works.

The instruments are discussed in the order in which they appear in the various works. Notes on horns, oboes, bassoon, violino piccolo, violone and the function of the harpsichord in continuo appear before the analysis of Concerto No. 1. The trumpet and recorder are discussed before Concerto No. 2; the recorder before Concerto No. 4; the flute before Concerto No. 5, and the gamba and viola da braccia before Concerto No. 6. I have not thought it necessary to describe the violin, viola or cello—they are, surely, too well known to be included in a book of this nature.

These Concertos have provided ground which has been dug over for a considerable number of years. Many people who know of Schweitzer, Spitta and Terry may not be aware of more recent work and research. I give below a short list of German publications which have appeared since the war:—

Sechs Brandenburgische Konzerte Kritischer Bericht by H. Besseler. 1956.

Beobachtungen am Autograph von Bachs Brandenburgischen Konzerten by P. Wackernagel. 1955.

Bach in Köthen by Fr. Smend. 1951.

Markgraf Christian Ludwig von Brandenburg by H. Besseler. 1956.

Bachs Brandenburgische Konzerte by R. Gerber. 1951.

Der Kapellmeister Bach by W. Vetter. 1950.

Zur Chronologie der Konzerte Joh. Seb. Bachs by H. Besseler. 1955.

Charakterthema und Erlebnisform bei Bach by H. Besseler. 1955.

It is my belief that not everyone, however interested he may be in the subject, has the time required for the detailed study which is necessary if such books as those mentioned are to yield their full value, and it is my hope that something more concise, and perhaps slightly controversial, may prove to be of interest to English-speaking readers.

The dates given for the composition of the concertos are those suggested by Heinrich Besseler in the excellent section devoted to 'Chronologie' in his *Sechs Brandenburgische Konzerte -Kritischer Bericht*.

ACKNOWLEDGEMENTS

My grateful thanks are due to the following for their kind advice, help and encouragement.

Philip Bate, Dennis Brain (the late), Eric Bravington, Harold Clarke, John Davis, Thurston Dart, F. C. Draper, Carl Dolmetsch, George Eskdale (the late), Roger Fiske, Ambrose Gauntlett, Charles Gregory, Ernest Hall, Geraint Jones, Philip Jones, Basil Lam, Eric McGavin, R. Morley-Pegge, Denis Stevens, August Wenzinger
and especially to my wife for her patience and forbearance!

CONTENTS

CONTENTS

LIST OF ILLUSTRATIONS

between pages 32-3

PART I

HISTORY

DEDICATION

In the early part of the year 1721 Bach sent a fair copy of six of his instrumental works to the Duke of Brandenburg. The actual month is not known. The dedication in the facsimile of the autograph score is not quite clear as to the final letter: it could be the 'r' of 'Mar.' or the 'i' of 'Mai.'

The dedication is a curious one and reads as follows:—

A Son Altesse Royalle
Monseigneur
Crêtien Louis
Marggraf de Brandenbourg etc. etc. etc.

Monseigneur,

Comme j'eus il y a une couple d'années, le bonheur de me faire entendre à Votre Altesse Royalle, en vertu de ses ordres, & que je remarquai alors, qu'Elle prennoit quelque plaisir aux petits talents que le Ciel m'a donnés pour la Musique, & qu'en prennant Congé de Votre Altesse Royalle, Elle voulut bien me faire l'honneur de me commander de Lui envoyer quelques pieces de ma Composition; j'ai donc selon ses tres gracieux ordres, pris la liberté de rendre mes tres-humbles devoirs à Votre Altesse Royalle, par les presents Concerts, que j'ai accommodés à plusiers Instruments; la priant tres-humblement de ne vouloir pas juger leur imperfection, à la riguer du gout fin et delicat, que tout le monde sçait qu'Elle a pour les pièces musicales; mais de tirer plutot en benigne Consideration, le profond respect, & la tres-humble obeissance que je tache à Lui temoigner par là. Pour le reste, Monseigneur, je supplie tres humblement Votre Altesse Royalle, d'avoir la bonté de continuer ses bonnes graces envers moi, et d'être persuadée que je n'ai rien tant à coeur, que de pouvoir être employé en des occasions plus dignes d'Elle et de son service, moi qui suis avec un zèle sans pareil,

Monseigneur,
De Votre Altesse Royalle,
Le tres humble & tres obeissant serviteur,
Jean Sebastian Bach

Coethen,d, 24 Ma(r)
1721.

A rough translation could be:—

Sir,

A couple of years ago I had the good fortune to perform before Your Royal Highness at Your command, and I noticed then that you showed some pleasure at the small talent for music which Heaven has given me. When I took my leave Your Royal Highness did me the great honour of ordering me to send Him some pieces of my own composition: therefore, and in accordance with His gracious order, I have taken the liberty of fulfilling my very humble duty to Your Royal Highness with these concerti which I have scored for several instruments.

Humbly I pray You not to judge their imperfections by the fine and delicate taste for music which everyone knows You possess, but rather to take into Your benign consideration the deep respect and very humble obedience which I have endeavoured to show You by them.

Further, Sir, I beg very humbly that Your Royal Highness will continue to have the goodness to hold me in His good favour and be convinced that I have nothing nearer to my heart than to be employed on occasions more worthy of You and Your service.

I am, Sir,
with unparalleled zeal,
Your Royal Highness's
Very humble and very obedient servant
Johann Sebastian Bach

Bach's comment 'a couple of years ago I had the good fortune to perform before Your Royal Highness at Your command . . .' leads us to suppose that he met the Duke of Brandenburg in Berlin towards the end of 1718 and played to him while there. The occasion of the visit was the purchase of a new keyboard instrument for Prince Leopold of Cöthen. The dedication quoted above seems to suggest that the Duke had expressed a wish to 'let me see some of your music sometime.' It does not, however, prove that the works so dedicated to the Duke were written especially for him and as a result of a direct or express commission. Indeed, there are many indications to the contrary:

1. From 1717 to 1723 Bach was employed by Prince Leopold of Anhalt-Cöthen. His duties were very largely secular as Leopold did not have music in his church services. The Prince, however, was a

keen musician and played violin, gamba and harpsichord. The Court orchestra was comparatively large—15 to 17 players in addition to Bach—and it was for this orchestra that Bach wrote the greater number of his instrumental works. It was not until 1729 when he was Director of the Telemann Musical Society in Leipzig that he had the opportunity or urge again to write purely secular instrumental music.

2. We know that Bach was a great experimenter, constantly trying out fresh instruments and instrumental combinations, and he would have had every facility and encouragement to do so with the Court orchestra, especially if he wrote something for one of the instruments played by the Prince!

3. We know that horn virtuosi travelled around in pairs and that two visited Cöthen for a few days in June, 1722 and, possibly, in September 1721 also. Terry, in his *Bach, a Biography* (page 122) refers to 'two Berlin musicians who were paid 36 thalers on September 19, 1721', and again in the same book (page 139) to an extract from the Cöthen accounts:— '*an die beyden Waldhornisten, so sich alhier hören lassen, 15 thaler.*' On the other hand, Besseler, in his *Sechs Brandenburgische Konzerte—Kritischer Bericht*' mentions that 'from time to time musicians (visiting) are noted in the (Cöthen) accounts; for instance, two waldhorn players in September 1721 and June 1722' One can accept such a statement from a Bach scholar of Besseler's imminence as being completely authoritative.

It is quite possible that Brandenburg Concerto No. 1, written a few years previously, had its first performances in the form which we know today during one or other of these visits, and one would like to think that, were he good enough, Leopold played the solo violin part. He may also have played the violin solos in Nos. 2 and 4, the gamba in No. 6 and the solo harpsichord in No. 5, leaving Bach to direct from the continuo harpsichord (although this, I believe, is unlikely. See comments on No. 5).

4. It seems logical to suppose that if Bach had accepted a commission from Brandenburg to write six works specifically for the latter's orchestra he would have found out what instruments were available and used them throughout, and not written six highly experimental works requiring widely differing resources. Bach was a practical man and, certainly when composing to order, unlikely to write for instruments which were unobtainable or unavailable.

The first version of the work known now as Concerto No. 1 was written in or about 1718. Is it possible or even probable that Bach would have written this work to include two instruments which his orchestra, i.e. the orchestra for which he was then engaged to provide music, did not possess and for which there were no players, in the expectation of having to wait, perhaps for years, for horn virtuosi to visit Cöthen and so make the work playable? I think it most improbable!

5. Bach re-used material from the Brandenburg concertos in later years which he would hardly have done had he regarded the works as exclusively the property of the Duke. If, however, he looked upon them merely as something he had written between 1717 and 1723 for no specific person then he might well have considered them as part of his musical capital on which he could draw as required.

The first movement of Concerto No. 1 in F serves as the Introduction to Cantata No. 52 dated around 1726 and entitled:— 'Falsche Welt, dir trau ich nicht.'

The third movement and the second Trio appear in the secular Cantata No. 207 'Vereinigte Zwietracht der wechselnden Saiten' of 1726 and in this Bach writes for three trumpets in place of the two horns of the original version.

The Sinfonia in F (Gesellschaft XXXI (1)) is another version of the first Concerto and is based on an earlier form (See BWV 1071). Did the original version, written for Leopold's orchestra, include parts for two trumpets and were these trumpets changed to jagdhorns for Brandenburg and did the two visiting hornists give the first performance of the *new* version which had been prepared for the Duke of Brandenburg?

Could it be that the movements which appear in Cantata 207 are not rearrangements of the Concerto material but similar to the original of 1718 and that the Concerto, which, as we know, had additional material added for Brandenburg, was in fact itself an arrangement?

The first movement of Concerto No. 3 in G serves as the first part of Cantata No. 174 dated 1729 and called:— 'Ich liebe den Höchsten von ganzem Gemüthe.' In this, Bach has added two oboes, taille, two corni da caccia and a bassoon to the original strings. It is possible that the last movement of this Concerto may have been derived from the last movement of the Pastorale in F, for organ, dating from between 1703 and 1707, i.e. the Arnstadt period.

Concerto No. 4 in G became the clavier concerto in F. (See BWV 1057).

There are at least two possible explanations regarding the choice of items sent to Brandenburg.

(i) That Bach wanted to give the Duke as wide a range of purely instrumental works as he could, or

(ii) that he had not bothered to find out anything of the composition of the Ducal orchestra and sent a selection of works in the hope that one or two would prove suitable.

One must, of course, choose the first alternative as Bach was seldom slapdash in his work unless extremely hard pressed for time and in this case he had had two years in which to obtain the necessary details. It will be agreed that he succeeded remarkably well.

Adam Carse, in the introduction to his 'The Orchestra in the 18th century' (published by W. Heffer and Sons Ltd) states:— 'When a Prince set up a musical establishment . . . he had to employ a Kapellmeister to compose music for him. He kept him for the purpose of supplying music . . . If an employer wanted a change of music, he commissioned another composer to write something for him and that composer wrote the pieces to order for a cash payment and for the exclusive use of the purchaser.' It is quite obvious that these conditions did not apply in Bach's case.

Of the six works he sent to the Duke, Nos. 1, 2, 4 and 5 are concerti grossi in the real sense, i.e. they have a small group of soloists (concertante) set against an accompanimental group (ripieno) with, of course, a continuo consisting of harpsichord and a bass string instrument (either cello or violone) to hold things together. No. 3 has no separate soloists and is, therefore, a concerto for orchestra. No. 6 is, in the author's opinion, not a concerto of any kind but a piece of pure chamber music written in the style of the period.

It should be noted that Bach himself did not call the works 'Brandenburg Concertos.' They bear the name for the same reason that certain of Beethoven's string quartets are called 'Rasoumovsky Quartets,' i.e. the name of their dedicatee makes a convenient handle and ready means of identification.

Carl Dolmetsch maintains that Bach's use of the word 'plusieurs' in his dedication gives the key to the whole problem of the performance of these works. ('. . . *par les presents Concerts que j'ai accomodes a plusieurs Instruments*') i.e. Concertos for several single instruments.

Harrap's Standard French and English Dictionary, 6th edition 1956, gives *plusieurs* as 'several' and *Nuttalls' Standard Dictionary* defines 'several' as 'separate, distinct, a few, single, various, taken singly'. If we accept this we are faced with the fact that Bach intended his ripieno parts to be played by one, or only a few, instruments to each line. This, in fact, is just what happens in Nos. 3 and 6 in ideal performances today. Strictly speaking, as there is no ripieno in No. 3 all the players are soloists and, of course, none of the parts in No. 6 should be doubled.

Bach himself, according to Spitta and Carl Philipp Emanuel, preferred to play the viola in the Cöthen band, but Dr Besseler, in his preface to the 1956 Bärenreiter edition of the Brandenburg Concertos, points out that in No. 5 the keyboard part was so important that Bach would certainly have taken it over; as the viola part was also indispensable, this would have been played by the second violinist, for whom no part is provided in this particular work. Spitta says (Vol II, page 68, English translation):— 'In his later years, too, he did not neglect his string playing, and in instrumental pieces in several parts he preferred to play the viola . . . good viola players, and such as satisfied his requirements, were seldom to be met with.'

BRANDENBURG'S ORCHESTRA

There is not much information available regarding the size and composition of the Ducal orchestra. It is known that Brandenburg had only six musicians in his service at the time of his death in 1734.

These were:—

Emmerling, composer, harpsichordist and gamba player
Kotowsky, flute (?)
Hagen, (?)
Kühltau, bassoon (?)
Emis, (?)
Ellinger, (?)

and it seems unlikely that his orchestra was much bigger during his lifetime.

Spitta, however, says:— (Vol II, page 129), 'How the offering (the Concertos) was received by the Markgraf is not known. His band was not lacking in members capable of executing these difficult works in a fit manner; we know the name of one of his private musicians. Emmerling, and that he was distinguished as a composer and performer on the Clavier and viol da gamba.'

LEOPOLD'S ORCHESTRA

Some details of Prince Leopold's orchestra at Cöthen are available and it seems to have been quite large.

Let us compare the known orchestra at Cöthen with a list of instruments actually required for the Concertos and consider how players could have 'doubled.'

THE ORCHESTRA AT CÖTHEN

Name	Instr.	1717	18	19	20	21	22	23
Speiss, Josephus	Vln.	1	1	1	1	1	1	1
Rose, Johann Ludwig	Oboe	1	1	1	1	1	1	1
Markus, Martin Friedrich	Vln.	1	1	1	1	1	½	–
Torlén, Johann Christoph	Fag.	1	1	1	1	1	1	1
Freytag, Johann Heinrich	Flute	1	1	1	1	–	–	–
Abel, Christian Ferdinand	Vln. & Gamba	1	1	1	1	1	1	1
Würdig, Johann Gottlieb	Flute	1	1	1	1	1	1	1
Linigke, Christian Bernhard	Cello	1	1	1	1	1	1	1
Fischer, Johann Valentin	(?)	–	–	½	1	1	1	1
Rolle, Christian	Vln. (?)	–	–	–	–	–	½	1
Freytag, Emanuel Heinrich Gottlieb	Flute (?)	–	–	–	–	1	1	1
Freytag, Johann	(?)	1	1	1	1	1	1	1
Harbordt, Wilhelm	(?)	1	–	–	–	–	–	–
Weber, Adam	(?)	1	–	–	–	–	–	–

Name	Instr.	1717	18	19	20	21	22	23
Freytag, E. H. G.	Flute (?)	1	1	1	1	–	–	–
Krahl, Johann Christoph	Trumpet	1	1	1	1	1	1	1
Schreiber, Johann Ludwig	Trumpet	1	1	1	1	1	1	1
Unger, Anton	Timps	1	1	1	1	1	1	1
Kräuser, Johann	Copyist	1	–	–	–	–	–	–
Göbel, Johann Bernhard	Copyist	–	1	–	–	–	–	–
Bach, Johann Bernhard	Copyist	–	1	½	–	–	–	–
Gottschalk, Emanuel Leberecht	Copyist	–	1	½	–	–	–	–
Vetter, Carl Friedrich	Copyist	–	–	½	1	1	1	1
		16	16	15	15	14	14	14

1 = present throughout the year.   ½ = part of the year only

The following list gives us the players and instruments (where known).

We have the Freytags, J. H. and

E. H. G.	flutes (?)
Rose	oboe
Torlén	bassoon
Krahl and Schreiber	} trumpets
Speiss, Markus and Rolle	} violins
Linigke	cello (and composer)
Abel	violin and gamba
. Unger	timpani

with Fischer, Freytag, J., Harbordt and Weber unaccounted for. Markus, who was a violinist, left the orchestra in June 1722 and was replaced by Rolle in the same month. It is, therefore, safe to assume that Rolle, also, was a violinist.

Freytag, J. H., died in 1721 and was replaced by Freytag, E. H. G., who was promoted.

Weber left in January 1718 and was not replaced.

Possibly Freytag, J., played second oboe and, perhaps, Harbordt or Weber was a viola. (Does their leaving the orchestra in 1718 explain why Bach played the viola, i.e. was it out of necessity as well as prediliction)?

The table which follows details the instruments required in each of the concertos.

Instrument	No. 1	2	3	4	5	6
Flute					I	
Recorder		I		2		
Oboe	3	I				
Bassoon	I					
Trumpet		I				
Horn	2					
Violin (piccolo)	I					
Violin (solo)		I		I	I	
Violin (orch. 1sts)	2	2	I	2	2	
Violin (orch. 2nds)	2	2	I	2		
Violin (orch. 3rds)			I			
Viola	2	2	3	2	2	2
Cello	I	I	3	I	I	I
Gamba						2
Violone	I	I	I	I	I	I
Harpsichord (solo and continuo)	I	I	I	I	I	I
	16	13	11	12	9	7

Points of interest arising from this analysis are:—

1) The flautist in Concerto No. 5 would certainly play the recorder in Nos. 2 and 4 and, possibly, 2nd oboe in No. 1 as well.

2) The 2nd recorder in No. 4 would, perhaps, play oboe in No. 1 and solo oboe in No. 2.

3) The 3rd oboe in No. 1 was, possibly, the 3rd viola in No. 3.

4) Likewise the bassoon in No. 1 could expect to play 3rd cello in No. 3 and 2nd gamba in No. 6.

5) Although players were expected to be able to double trumpet and horn and vice versa it is possible that Leopold's pair of trumpeters, being court musicians, would feel the playing of a mere hunting instrument to be beneath their dignity. If this is so then all performances of the work which took place in Cöthen prior to 1721 or 1722 would, probably, have been with trumpets, and the horn

version which we are used to hearing today might not have been played until a pair of travelling virtuosi visited the court in the years just mentioned.

6) If the 3rd oboe player in No. 1 did not play 3rd viola in No. 3 it is possible that the 2nd violin took 3rd viola. (In his Leipzig days Bach liked 3 first and 3 second violins—(when he could get them)— but this figure would be rather on the generous side even for a Princely Court and Brandenburg, probably had to be content with 1 first and 1 second).

7) The piccolo violin of No. 1 and the solo violin of Nos. 2, 4 and 5 would be one and the same player. (But perhaps not Leopold).

8) The two cellists would change over to 1st gamba and cello for No. 6 leaving the bassoonist/3rd cello to sustain the 2nd gamba line —or did Leopold play it?

9) It is unlikely that a second keyboard player was available for the continuo harpsichord as opposed to the concertante harpsichord in No. 5, and one player would have to fulfil both functions.

In the light of these considerations the composition of the orchestra was probably as follows:—

2 flutes doubling recorders and oboes	2
1 oboe doubling 3rd viola	1
1 bassoon doubling 2nd gamba	1
2 trumpets	2
3 first violins	3
2 second violins	2
2 violas	2
2 cellos, one doubling gamba	2
1 violone	1
1 keyboard player	1
	17

The number of players in the orchestra, however, never exceeded sixteen with the addition of Bach himself. They were divided into three groups; first, eight or nine players who were described as 'chamber musicians'; second, between two and four players who were 'musicians' and a third consisting of two trumpets, a timpanist and a copyist. Three people were employed in the latter capacity during part of 1718 and 1719.

Some of the 'chamber musicians' may have held comparatively light domestic jobs (secretaries, valets, etc.) in the Princely household and the 'musicians' were, perhaps, a little lower in the social scale—lackeys, cooks, gardeners, etc. It is unlikely that the trumpeters and timpanists held other posts as they would have to play at many Court functions apart from the evening orchestral session; and, bearing in mind the amount of music written by Bach in these six years, one can imagine that the copyist was kept more than busy.

Let us see how many musicians would be required to perform the works with single players to a part.

	No. 1	2	3	4	5	6
Flute					1	
Recorder		1		2		
Oboe	3	1				
Bassoon	1					
Trumpet		1				
Horn	2					
Violin piccolo	1					
Violin solo		1		1	1	
Violin orch. 1st	1	1	1	1	1	
Violin orch. 2nd	1	1	1	1		
Violin orch. 3rd			1			
Viola	1	1	3	1	1	2
Cello	1	1	3	1	1	1
Gamba						2
Violone	1	1	1	1	1	1
Harpsichord	1	1	1	1	1	1
	13	10	11	9	7	7

Allowing for the fact that the two horns in No. 1 were visitors, we see that not more than eleven (resident) players were required for any of the concertos. In this way the more fumble-fingered of the cooks, gardeners and coachmen could be left out of the orchestra on the occasions when these particular works were played, and the performance left in the safer hands of the more skilled or 'professional' musicians.

It is interesting to note that Bach started off this particular collection of concertos with a tremendous flourish, using every instrumentalist likely to be found in the Court for No. 1 and scoring each work for ever decreasing forces. Did he do this in view of the fact that the Duke's orchestra was smaller than we have assumed and that he could not expect 'extras' to be engaged—or even found—for more than one of the set?

It is known that Bach considered the horn, especially the Jagd-horn, as an instrument of salutation and obviously thought it fitting that a pair should be used in the 1st concerto—or, rather, the concerto now numbered as 1— as it was a tribute to the Nobility, i.e. the Duke. (See Terry, *Bach's Orchestra* page 46, 'Its notes, by long tradition, were the salute of Princes').

I   This cor de chasse or corno da caccia is dated about 1800 but there is little difference between it and one made 100 years earlier— the width of the bell in the later model might be a little more and the metal may be slightly thicker in gauge.   *Reproduced by kind permission of Boosey & Hawkes.*

2 The shorter of the two oboes on the left was made by I. C.
Denner of Nürnberg prior to 1700. The other is by T. Stanesby
senior, of London. It, also, was built before 1700. They are both in
Mr. Philip Bate's collection and the photographs are reproduced
by his permission. *Right* Two Dutch Oboes. (*i*) (*Left*) This oboe, dated
1695, is by C. Rijkel, of Amsterdam. (*ii*) (*Right*) This is a tenor oboe
of the early 1700's made by R. Wyne, of Nijmegen. Loan Dienst
voor's Ryks Verspreide Kunstvoorweipen to the Haags Gemeinte-
museum. *Reproduction by permission of the Director. Copyright reserved.*

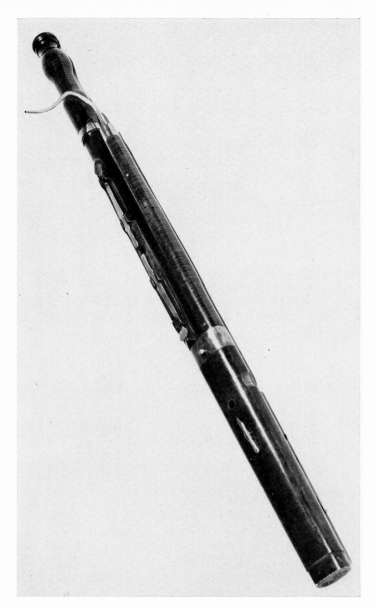

3 Although this bassoon dates from 50 or 60 years after the Brandenburg period there is little to choose between it and an earlier instrument so far as key mechanism is concerned. The later instrument might be a little lighter and better finished and, possibly, smoother tonally, otherwise it is very similar to that used by Bach's players. *Reproduced by kind permission of Boosey & Hawkes.*

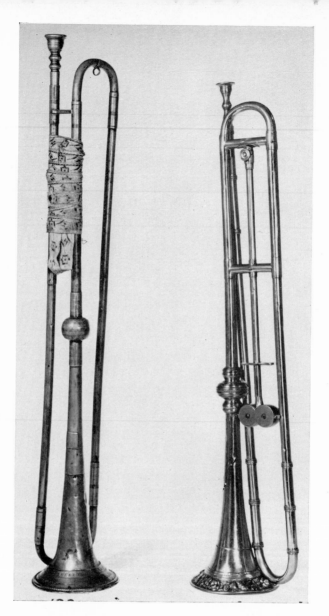

4 This is a fine specimen of tromba da tirarsi or slide trumpet. In it, the slide operates against the pull of a spring housed in the two circular 'pill boxes'. Much more convenient and easy to manipulate than the older type of trumpet wherein the slide (set between the mouthpiece and the main body of the instrument) operated somewhat similarly to a trombone with a single slide tube. *Reproduced by kind permission of Boosey & Hawkes.* It is interesting to compare this natural trumpet of about 1770 having one fold, with the Schmidt instrument of 1772 with a double fold. Assuming the 1770 instrument to be in the same key (F) as the Schmidt there is no appreciable difference in total length of tubing, but a great deal in convenience of handling. *Reproduced by kind permission of Boosey & Hawkes.*

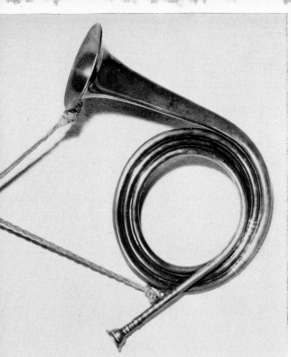

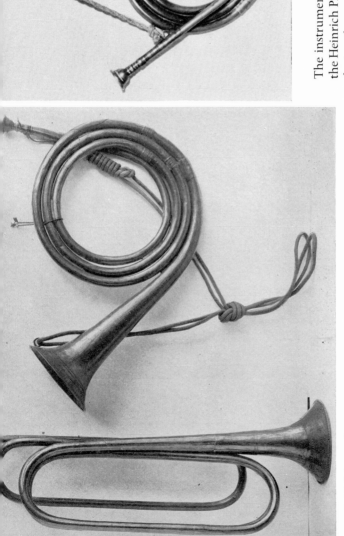

5 Folded (natural) trumpet in F made by J. J. Schmidt of Pfaffendorf in 1772—fifty years after the Brandenburgs were written. Jagd-trompete (curled) made by Heinrich Pfeifer, of Leipzig, in 1697, (twenty years before Bach moved to Cöthen). The instrument was in the Musikinstrumenten-Museum of the Karl-Marx-Universität, Leipzig; unfortunately it was destroyed in the last war but, luckily the Museum authorities had the foresight to make a copy. This photograph, together with that of the Schmidt trumpet, is reproduced by kind permission of Mr. R. Morley-Pegge to whom the originals belong.

The instrument shown in this photograph is a copy of the Heinrich Pfeifer trumpet (1697) which was destroyed during the war. It is interesting to compare it with the photo of the original instrument shown in 5b. Reproduction is by courtesy of the Custodian of the Musikinstrumenten-Museum of the Karl-Marx-Universität, Leipzig. The photograph is by Foto-Clauss, also of Leipzig.

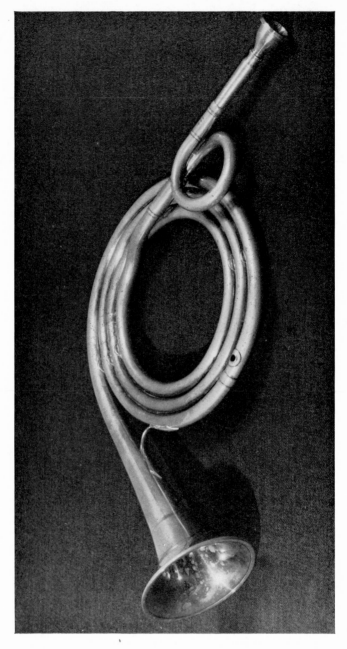

6 The clarino trumpet shown above is the property of Mr. Philip James. The photograph is reproduced by his permission.

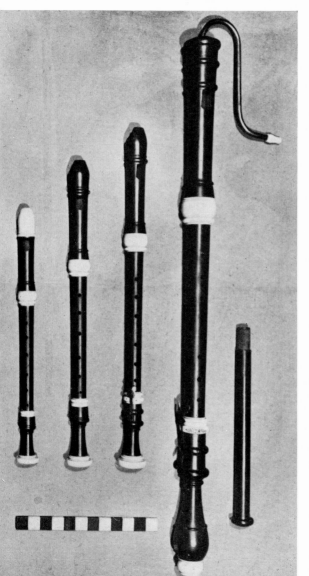

7 This set of four recorders, Treble, Alto, Tenor and Bass (complete with peg) was made by Bressan in the 18th Century and is, therefore, contemporary with the Brandenburg Concertos. The set is the property of the Grosvenor Museum, Chester, and the photograph is reproduced by kind permission of the Chief Education Officer, Chester.

8   This one-keyed flute (traverso) is dated circa 1690. It is one
of a type which was in constant use throughout Europe early in
the 18th century. The name Rippert is stamped on all three
sections of the instrument which is number '42-68ak in the Glen
Collection, Kelvin Grove Art Gallery and Museum, Glasgow.
The photograph is reproduced by permission of the Director.
The curved cor anglais dates from the early 1700's, i.e., Bach's
Cöthen or even Weimar period. It is therefore, the type of instrument on which his colleague in the Court orchestra would have
played.

PART II

INSTRUMENTS AND ANALYSIS

CHAPTER I

BRANDENBURG CONCERTO
No. 1

JAGDHORN

A natural (hunting) horn pitched in F and having a total length of approximately 12 feet contains the following notes in its harmonic series: (actual sounds)

The two notes under 11 and the two under 13 are rather vague. Lip pressure can bring them almost in tune in a slow moving passage but a fast one gives no time for adjustment and the listener's ear has to accept what comes.

The notes required by Bach in Concerto No. 1 are these (1st horn stems up, 2nd horn stems down):

(written notes)

It will be noticed that the 1st horn is spared the 3rd and 7th harmonics and the 2nd does not have to play the 14th, 15th and 16th. Both players have to do their best with the two notes possible from the 11th harmonic.

OBOE

The oboe, as Bach knew it, dates back to about 1655. It was a conical tube with eight holes and a compass of just over two octaves extending from middle C. Six of the holes were open and to be covered by the player's fingers, the other two were covered by square-headed brass keys. The opening of the lowest hole (large brass key) gave the note ♪ *Ex. 3.* and the next key *Ex. 4.* but the only method of obtaining the

C-sharp/D-flat was to half open the large key so that the player blew either a very sharp C or a very flat D!

Bach uses three oboes in Concerto No. 1 and requires these notes from the first player:

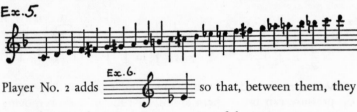

Ex. 5.

Player No. 2 adds *Ex. 6.* so that, between them, they

cover the complete chromatic compass of the instrument.

A delightful book called *The Modern Music-Master or the Universal Musician,* published in Bow Church Yard in 1731, contains, amongst other treasures, 'Instructions Upon the Hautboy, in a more Familiar Method than any extant'.

The 'Instructions' open as follows:

'First observe the manner of holding your Hautboy which is this, place your left hand uppermost next to your mouth and your right hand below: though there are eight holes on this Instrument besides two under ye Brass Keys making ten in all, nevertheless seven fingers will be sufficient to supply them, as for Example, Let the forefinger of your left hand cover the first hole, the second finger the second and the third finger the next two holes. In like manner the forefinger of your right hand must stop the next two holes, then place the second finger of the same hand on the next hole together with the third finger on the lowest hole in view and your little finger will command the biggest brass key, so that by setting it down pretty hard it will cover the lowest hole.

'Thus all the Holes of your Pipe being stopt, blow somewhat

strong and you will distinctly hear C which is the lowest Note on the Hautboy'.

N.B. the 'biggest brass key' when pressed (or 'set down pretty hard') *covered* the hole under it but the 'lesser brass key' was to *uncover* its hole when pressed. '. . . your little finger must be set on the lesser brass key which lifts that off from the hole'.

The fingering chart given in the book is as follows:

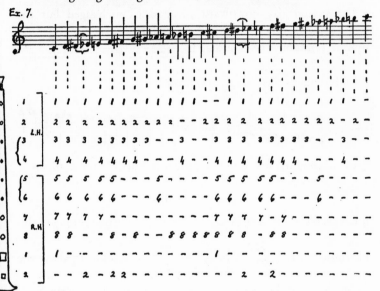

Ex. 7.

Notice that one fingering serves for D-sharp and E-flat but that there is a difference between G-sharp and A-flat.

BASSOON
(Referred to in Concerto No. 1 as 'Bassono')

Bach nearly always used a bassoon when his orchestra contained three oboes. The instrument was required not only to support the continuo but also as a bass, sometimes independent of the basso continuo, to the oboe trio. (See, too, Cantata No. 174 of 1729, in which the Sinfonia is another version of the first movement of Brandenburg Concerto No. 3 in G).

The instrument, more or less in its present-day form, that is, with two conical, parallel, wooden tubes inserted into a junction box, dates back to about 1655—the year which saw (or heard), the debut of the oboe basically as we know it today—or earlier. It had eleven finger holes, three being covered by keys and its compass was from

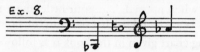

The present-day downward compass is unchanged but the upward limits have been pushed to

Bach requires these notes in Concerto No. 1:

thus avoiding the low B-flat and the top fourth of the compass.

VIOLINO PICCOLO

It has been suggested by Praetorious that the normal tuning of this instrument was

i.e. a fourth above the ordinary violin, but examination of the score of Concerto No. 1 shows that Bach wrote for an instrument tuned a minor third above the normal, so: and regarded it as a transposing instrument, its part being written in D, the opening passage, written so:

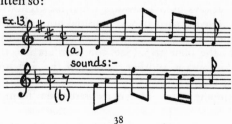

Some of the chordal passages which look quite possible as written in D take on a very different aspect when transposed into F so that the part may be played on a violin with normal tuning, e.g.

Present day violinists will not need to be reminded that the E minor chord in bar 2 of B is quite a handful compared with the same bar in A.

Further references to the instrument are made on pages 46 and 47 when the horn is discussed.

VIOLONE

This instrument is a six-stringed bass-gamba tuned an octave lower

than the gamba, i.e., its lowest note is

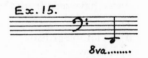

(see page 106). It has a soft, clear tone, not so boomy as the average double-bass which is the bass of the violin family. The violone is usually considered as being the bass of the viols and, therefore, as having a fretted fingerboard.

Reference to the facsimile autograph score of the Concertos published by Peters of Leipzig shows that Bach experimented with the instruments constituting the lower line as follows:

In ripieno		In continuo
No. 1 has cello	and	violone grosso
No. 2 has violone	and	cello and basso
No. 3 has		basso
No. 4 has violone	and	cello
No. 5 has		cello and violone
No. 6 has cello	and	violone

This seems to suggest that either he was unable to make up his mind as to which instrument provided the ideal bass to the ripieno and continuo or that he was experimenting with tone colour. This variety in instruments is very understandable where his church cantatas are concerned as he seldom knew from one week to the next what instruments would be available for the following Sunday; hence he had to use cello, violone, gamba, trombone, bassoon, string bass, or organ as and when he could. One cannot think that he laboured under this disability at Cöthen however and so can but assume that he liked to ring the changes.

Terry (see page 121 of his *Bach's Orchestra*) says: 'There is no positive evidence that he employed the contrabass. The term "contrabass" refers here to the "Gross Quint-Bass" a five-stringed instrument

tuned _____ and mentioned by Praetor-

ious in his *Tabella Universalis*. But the score of "Was mir behagt" (a secular cantata (No. 208) dated 1716) prescribes a "Violone Grosso".'

The accounts of St. Thomas' Church in Leipzig show that a 'large' violone was bought at an auction in 1735 or 1736.

As we have seen from the autograph Bach refers to:

a) a violone
b) a violone grosso
c) a basso

and immediately we are faced with a problem. We know that the

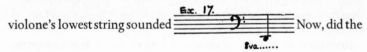

violone's lowest string sounded _____ Now, did the

violone *grosso* go even lower or was Bach referring to one and the same instrument under different names?

In seeming contradiction to his statement on page 121 Terry says on page 153 'That a contrabass was occasionally at his disposal is suggested by the apparent existence of a part in the St. John Passion of 1723 and the secular cantata "Was mir behagt"!'

On page 4 of his book he gives the composition of the orchestra at Weimar, of which Bach was a member from 1708-1717, i.e., including the time when he wrote 'Was mir behagt'. The list includes the name of Joh. Andreas Ehrbach, described as 'Violonist' and

'Kunstcammerer' (Superintendent of the Art Museum). If Terry's statement on page 153 is correct one is left to wonder (1) if Ehrbach borrowed a contrabass in 1716 (perhaps while his violone was under repair) or (2) if a contrabass player visited the Court while Ehrbach was on leave or sick or (3) did Bach, in a moment of forgetfulness, write' contrabass' when he meant 'violone basso'?

In a memorandum dated August 1730 which he sent to the authorities at Leipzig, Bach declares that he needs 'two violoncellists and one violone player'. Note that he does not mention contrabass, also that he seemed to have to wait until 1735 or 1736 to obtain a violone even though he may have had a player available before that.

CONTINUO

In the eighteenth century the musician who played the harpsichord continuo quite often directed the orchestra also and was responsible for the performance. Therefore he had to be placed in the centre of the orchestra where he could be seen by all the players and heard by as many as possible. Exceptions to this were provided by famous violinist leaders like Corelli, who directed his orchestra from his leader's desk and relegated the harpsichord continuo player to a comparatively lowly position. This, unfortunately, is in accordance with the present-day practice, as seen in some orchestras, of placing the harpsichord at the side of the stage somewhere at the back of the first fiddles. This, of course, is quite ridiculous as, (1) the player becomes just another member of the orchestra and (2) he is inaudible to almost everyone—including the audience!

The ideal method was that adopted by Thurston Dart with the Philomusica Orchestra where all the players were clustered around the centrally placed harpsichord. Those instrumentalists most vitally concerned, i.e., the 1st violin, 1st cello plus cello or violone (double bass these days, alas!) continuo were nearest to him.

The style or type of continuo required is highly debatable. C. P. E. Bach in his book states that the main function of the continuo player is to keep time and fill in harmony and J. S. Bach, in one of his own worked basses or written-out continuos (see Terry's *Bach's Orchestra* page 170) shows that the right hand part should be simple and harmonic rather than florid and melodic.

The part should, of course, be played on a harpsichord whenever possible. A piano is a very poor second best.

ANALYSIS

Concerto No. 1 in F à

2 Corni di Caccia ⎫
3 Hautbois é Bassono ⎬Concertanti
Violino Piccolo Concertato ⎭

2 Violini ⎫
una Viola è Violincello ⎬Ripieno
Col Basso Continuo ⎭

In its original form this concerto dated from about 1717 or even earlier. It was lengthened and revised to become the work we know so well today around 1720.

It was very near the three-movement form of the other concertos when first written and consisted of an Allegro, an Adagio and a Finale comprising a Menuetto with Trios I and II. The Allegro third movement and Polonaise were added later.

What is more important than its shape is the fact that it was not conceived as a concerto grosso but as a work for orchestra in which there was no concertante versus ripieno. Bach does not appear to have become interested in concerti-grossi as such until rather later in his career. Besseler is of the opinion that the form was in the composer's thoughts when, towards the end of 1718, he was in touch with the Duke of Brandenburg.

In his early days, however, his compositions show no particular contrast between solo or soli and tutti. Brandenburg No. 6 which, so far as we know, was written before any of the other works in the collection, is an excellent example. The same applies to Nos. 3 and 1 in its original form. The music was for communal playing and pleasure.

The division of No. 1 into soli and accompanimental groups, and the addition of a part for solo violino piccolo, took place at the time when the extra movements were written into the score.

For purposes of analysis we must re-divide Bach's forces into four groups, thus:

1) the two corni di caccia

2) the three oboes

3) the violins (including solo), violas and cello

4) the violone, bassoon and harpsichord continuo.

The bassoon is treated as a continuo instrument except on certain occasions which will be noted later.

First Movement (Allegro).

We need to discuss the first three groups only so far as the thematic layout is concerned. Each group has its own distinctive and characteristic theme which becomes almost an identity disc or label. Before, however, going any further with our analysis we must try to decide on the type of brass instrument Bach required.

The Concerto opens with two traditional hunting calls and closes with another. In call No. 1 the first horn enters a bar after the second without waiting for its player to finish his flourish. The result is rather a jumble rhythmically although it is clear enough on paper.

(written notes, horn in F)

Ex.18.

Note that the (sounded) notes given on page 35 are for an ordinary horn pitched in F, but some scholars are of the opinion that horns in F alt were used so that the sounded notes were a fourth *above* the written—i.e., an octave higher than those given in the example.

There are several grounds for this point of view.

1) H. C. Robbins Landon, in his monumental work *The Symphonies of Joseph Haydn* (1955) says, (pages 334/5): 'Until Symphony 51, Haydn seems to have concentrated exclusively on the brilliant high register of the horn . . .'

He certainly concentrated on the high register with a will, for in the Adagio (2nd movement) of Symphony 51 he gives this passage to the 1st horn:

(Actual sounds, written for horn in E-flat, i.e. sounding a 6th below the written notes)

Ex.19.

and, in the trio to the minuet:

(Actual sounds, written for horn in B-flat Alt., i.e. sounding a tone below the written notes)

Ex.20.

This work was written between 1771 and 1774—rather more than fifty years later than the Brandenburgs and when Haydn was about 40 years of age (he was 18 at the time of Bach's death in 1750). Landon's remark suggests that one should examine the style of horn writing of other composers working in Germany or Austria at a somewhat earlier period than Haydn's. It must be remembered that Haydn went to the Esterhazy Court in May 1761 where he was in charge of an orchestra of sixteen players. Although so young at the time of Bach's death it is probable that he knew some of the earlier Master's work. I think we can accept as a fact that if horn parts were played 'in alt' at the Court of Esterhazy the same practice would operate in other European Princely and Ducal Court orchestras. The question arises, when did this practice begin? It is not something which could happen at the turn of a switch nor at a given date by Royal decree. One cannot, for example, imagine Count Esterhazy or some other Princeling having a memo pinned on to the notice board in his band room to the effect that 'as from 1st January, 17.. all horn parts will be played an octave higher than hitherto'! Therefore it is logical to suppose that this type of playing had been evolved and had become standard over a period of years. The following extract from *Grove's Dictionary* (1954 edition) is of interest. 'Bach, Handel and other composers of that time did not hesitate to write high, florid parts for horns precisely similar in character to the contemporary trumpet parts. Such parts, in the light of present-day technique, now try our very best players to the limit of their capacity, but to those of Bach's day, most, if not all of them, trained trumpeters who only took over the horn when required, the technique was that of the clarino, whose range was confined to the two upper octaves and was never carried below the 4th harmonic'.

If we accept this theory regarding Bach's horn parts then the corno da caccia obbligato to 'Quoniam' in the B minor Mass, which

is written out in the treble clef and goes up to

in the new Bärenreiter edition of the work, should be played to sound at the written pitch and would need to be played on a piccolo horn or trumpet in D today.

2) Brass players were expected to be equally proficient on trumpet, horn and trombone. Players employed by the municipality and known as 'Stadtpfeifern' were expected to play violin, oboe, traverso, trumpet, horn and other wind instruments. Carl Friedrich Pfaffe, who was auditioned by Bach in 1745, played all these. We are told that in 1750 a candidate for a Stadtpfeifer post failed on trumpet, horn and oboe. Without ability on these instruments in addition to several others he could not become a Stadtpfeifer. In 1769 two candidates for similar jobs were expected to play violone, all four trombones (discant, alto, tenor and bass), violin, slide trumpet, horn or oboe and flute including concerti for the two latter instruments!

Where the trumpet and horn were concerned, only a change of quality and not of pitch was required. This change of quality or tone-colour could, perhaps, be obtained by using the same instrument with a modified mouthpiece, i.e., a very shallow cup for the high trumpet quality or colour and a more conical cup for the horn colour.

3) Yet another ground for thinking that Bach was writing for horns in alt is the general layout of the music.

The three oboes constitute a closely-knit family, thus:

So, also, do the strings:

(note that after the first half bar they are almost in unison with the three oboes). Notice too the mixture of harmonies on the fourth

quaver beat of the first bar: i.e. tonic and

dominant sounding at the same time.

The horn calls referred to earlier on are thrust into the midst of this sound mass if they are played at normal F pitch but rise above it if played in F in alt (see Ex 25) and, in fact, reinforce the 1st oboe and 1st violin to a great extent

(Horn notes are diamond shape).

This is even more noticeable in the third (Allegro) movement where, commencing at the 30th bar, the solo (piccolo) violin and the 1st horn play as follows (actual sounds):

If we regard the quavers in the first half bar of the horn part and the second half bar of the violin line as being accompaniment to each other's semiquaver passages it will be seen that a state bordering on chaos reigns. If, on the other hand, the horn part sounds an octave higher, both parts are beautifully clear. It must be remembered, too, that the piccolo violin was very weak in tone and could not possibly have battled successfully with horn tone as we know it in its own register. Mr Nap de Klijn, the well-known

Dutch violinist, told me some time ago that he had taken part in a performance of this work playing a three-quarter size violin tuned up a minor third, i.e. to B-flat, F, C and G. This—the correct tuning for a piccolo violin in this work—made the three and four-part chordal passages quite playable but the instrument was practically inaudible and he had been quite unable to hear himself both in the passage just referred to and in many others.

The fact that Bach used the third movement of No. 1 as the basis of the first chorus in the secular cantata 'Vereinigte Zwietracht der wechselnden Saiten' transposed down into the key of D and with trumpets in place of horns shows that he did not dislike the sound of high brass in this work!

This passage, for instance, bears out my contention:

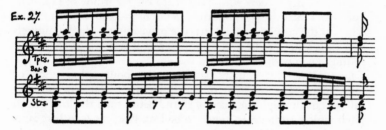

i.e. that the two parts need to be spaced apart so that the shape and detail is clear. And this version of the Trio II (in the same secular cantata) makes the point even clearer as the parts are more widely spread. (See, also, Ex 37).

Years ago I was a member of the BBC Symphony Orchestra at the same time as the late Aubrey Brain, the famous horn virtuoso. I well remember an incident which interested me very much at the time and which has intrigued me even more since.

During the lunch interval between two rehearsal sessions a member of the orchestra bought a toy horn. It was a 'natural' instrument in that it had no valves. It was, presumably, made of tin, was about the size of an old F crook and had a shallow cup mouthpiece with a wide rim like a post horn which flared out into a bell about five or six inches across.

This was presented to Aubrey who promptly removed the mouthpiece, inserted his own horn mouthpiece and proceeded to play all the well-known flourishes suitable for a natural instrument —in high trumpet register but with a *horn tone quality*! What is more, the instrument was soft in dynamic and would have balanced a recorder or oboe perfectly. I feel that if a little toy like this, costing about three to five shillings, could do the trick then a properly built instrument made of the correct materials should do so even better. (See page 66).

Those of my readers who have heard the recording of Brandenburg No. 1 made by the Philomusica Orchestra and Thurston Dart wherein the corni da caccia parts are played on two high trumpets will realise how right and logical some, if not all, of the music sounds when performed in this way.

One cannot, of course, be dogmatic about either pitch or instrument. The trumpet pitch allows the fanfares or hunting calls to cut through the mass of sound better than the lower horn pitch which, sometimes, tends to be lost. Passages as in bars 24, 25 and 26 become more shapely if the bar 24 entry is of high pitch. Bars 40 and 41 give one a choice. Did Bach want the octave jump between the horns and 1st and 2nd oboes, so:

or did he want notes of the same pitch, thus:

Bars 53 and 54 provide another little puzzle. If trumpet pitch is used the brass entry (in thirds) is followed by a similar passage (also in thirds) between brass (top notes) and 1st oboe and then by the same passage (still in thirds) between piccolo violin (top notes) and 1st oboe, but now the brass entry—if at high pitch—is a sixth above the piccolo violin!

This, as we see, gives us three statements in thirds and one in sixths. On the other hand, if horn pitch is used the first (horn) entry (in thirds) is followed by sixths between 1st oboe (top notes) and 1st horn, then by thirds between piccolo violin and 1st oboe and again by thirds between piccolo violin (top notes) and 1st horn, i.e. an entry in thirds, one in sixths and two more in thirds. In neither case can we be consistent with all thirds or else thirds and sixths alternating.

Bars 69 and 70, which correspond with bars 40 and 41, do not help us in the least as the brass passage can be either a third below or a sixth above the string answer and not a unison or octave jump as earlier in the movement.

The Menuetto is a problem too, as, with the exception of the last three bars, the brass is used purely to fill in. It sounds perfectly correct at horn pitch but rather ridiculous if, for example in bars 17–21, it rises right above the strings and oboes.

I may appear to have argued both sides of the question but must admit that there is little concrete evidence available for one or the other. We are, it would seem, more or less justified in using the pitch we like and the tone colour we prefer—I don't think Bach would mind. In 1721—the dedication year—Bach asked for corni da caccia and in that year or 1722 two players visited Cöthen and played the Concerto. In 1726 in the 'Dramma per Musica' 'Vereinigte Zwietracht der wechselnden Saiten', Bach goes back to 'tromba', i.e. trumpets (third movement (Allegro) and 2nd Trio) and in 1730 in the Cantata No. 52, 'Falsche Welt, dir trau ich nicht', he demands corni (Waldhorns). Let us, therefore, try to sum up:

49

D

1. *For Trumpets,*

a) Trumpets, or instruments of trumpet pitch, sound well in the 1st movement although, as I have pointed out in my detailed analysis, the actual layout of the notes does not confirm that Bach had this pitch in mind.

b) There were no horn players in Leopold's orchestra at the time when No. 1 was written and it is possible that the Court trumpeters would feel slighted if asked to play a mere hunting instrument.

c) Trumpets sound very well in the 3rd movement and the raising of the pitch of the brass instruments an octave clears some of the semiquaver passages from the violin piccolo register—thus making for clarity in part-writing.

d) Trumpet pitch makes Trio II extremely brilliant and exciting and, again, takes the brass notes out of the register of the accompaniment.

2. *For Horns,*

a) The introduction of hunting fanfares into the musical text suggests a hunting instrument (i.e. horn) rather than a Court instrument (e.g. trumpet).

b) Although Brandenburg No. 1 was not composed first it is written out as the first of the collection and, therefore, may be taken as a salute. Bearing in mind the remark that the horn is the instrument of Nobility, the use of the instrument in this work would seem logical.

c) Trumpet pitch sounds absolutely wrong in the Menuet. On the other hand the extreme simplicity of the brass writing in this movement could suggest that trumpeters (although inexperienced as hornists) were being asked to fill in the lower harmonies.

On page 45 I pointed out that a change of colour as between horn and trumpet could, perhaps (and one must underline the 'perhaps'), be obtained by a change of mouthpiece. This, of course, is a controversial subject and one upon which it is almost impossible to pronounce.

Theoretically the tone quality of a brass instrument is determined by the size of the bore and the rate of taper with slight variations due to the different materials used. The mouthpiece is a means of collecting the vibrations of the player's lips and conveying them to the air within the tube. The shape and depth of the mouthpiece cup should be relative to the bore of the particular instrument for which it is intended and, in addition, must be related to the player's approach to sound production, i.e. it must fit his embouchure and be generally 'comfortable'.

On the other hand, players of the calibre of the Brains (Aubrey and Dennis), could make vast changes of quality with different mouthpieces. One hears that certain trumpet players in German orchestras use special mouthpieces with detachable and inter-changeable cups of varying degrees of shallowness which are designed to enable the player to modify his tone quality according to the period and the style of the composition he is playing and assist him to produce sounds in the particular register required.

Having considered the problem of pitch on musical grounds let us see what the laws of acoustics have to say on the subject.

We have seen (on page 35) that an instrument of approximately twelve feet in length will give all the notes demanded by Bach in Concerto No. 1—notes, that is, at the pitch we are used to. A twelve-foot instrument bent into a double circle would have a diameter of about twenty inches, i.e. rather more than a present-day horn and it is logical to suppose that it would be held in traditional hunting horn manner. The player's right arm would be roughly parallel with the ground. His hand would grasp that part of the instrument's circumference lying farthest from the lip and the near portion of the circumference would rest on the player's forearm. Thus the bell of the instrument would point, more or less, over the player's right shoulder.

An instrument of six feet in length would have its harmonic series pitched an octave higher and would sound as in Thurston Dart's recent recordings (see page 48). When given two curls it would have a diameter of about ten inches or, if having four curls, about five inches—and, in fact, would look extremely like the instrument pictured in Hausmann's painting of the famous Bach trumpeter, Gottfried Reiche, which many readers will have seen in various books on Bach and his music. There is a reproduction of it in Terry's *Bach's Orchestra*.

A little exercise in subdivision will show that if a horn in F (usual pitch) is twelve feet in length and a horn in high F is six feet long then:

a horn in G will be approximately 11 feet in length

a horn in A will be approximately 10 feet in length

a horn in B-flat will be approximately 9½ feet in length

a horn in C will be approximately 8½ feet in length

a horn in D will be approximately 7½ feet in length

a horn in E-flat will be approximately 7 feet in length

a horn in F will be approximately 6 feet in length

The section on trumpets on pages 61 to 66 refers to the instrument shown in Hausmann's painting and mentions that accurate measurements suggested it to have been in D and fitted with a C crook. Our table shows that if in D it would have to measure about seven and a half feet in length and that the C crook would be about twelve inches so giving a total length of approximately eight feet six inches.

All we can learn from a short study of the harmonic law, therefore, is that if Bach wanted the horn parts in No. 1 to sound at the pitch we are used to then the players must have used twelve foot instruments and that if he wanted tham to sound an octave higher six foot instruments were required. In the former case the players would, no doubt, have held them as already described and in the latter they could have handled them as Gottfried Reiche does and played them as he appears about to do.

N.B. I have given measurements as 'approximately' or 'about'. This is because, where the six and twelve foot lengths are concerned, no account has been taken of 'end-correction', i.e. I have given the length of the tubing required for a given note or harmonic series and not the length of the actual column of air most of which is enclosed within the tube.

A small amount of the vibrating air column protrudes beyond the end of the bell—the amount of protrusion varying with the size and bore of the instrument, e.g. a B-flat tuba has an end-correction or protrusion of approximately ten inches. Accurate calculation can determine the exact length which a vibrating column of air is required to have to produce a given note. If a tube be made of an exactly similar length the note produced by it will be flatter than that chosen originally, as the anti-node, or 'free end', of the air column opposite the node or mouthpiece will be slightly beyond the actual end of the tube. Therefore a tube must always be shorter than the length of the air column required for a given note by the amount of the end-correction. This correction length may be found as follows:

Select a point as near to the end of the bell of the instrument as possible and which forms an angle of not more than forty-five degrees with the axis, thus:

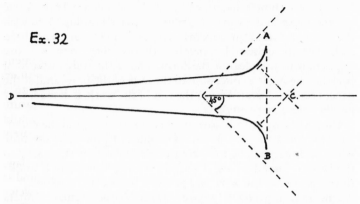

Ex. 32

Drop a perpendicular at right angles from it and do the same from a point exactly opposite. The spot where these two lines bisect will be the anti-node.

The line A—B represents the end of the instrument but the point C is the anti-node or 'free-end' of the vibrating air column. That portion of the line C—D which extends beyond the line A—B is the 'end-correction'.

It should be emphasized that the method I have described is very rough and ready and while giving fairly accurate results with modern instruments is apt to be rather wide of the mark when dealing with seventeenth and eighteenth century models with their very small and narrow bells.

The view that Concerto No. 1 was a three-movement work in its original form is, I think, beginning to be accepted by scholars and musicologists. It consisted of the ¼ Allegro, the ¾ Adagio and the Menuetto with two Trios and was, in fact, practically identical with the Sinfonia in F (BG XXXI (I)) (BWV 1071) and dated by Schmieder as 'around 1730'. There is no part for the piccolo violin (tutti first violins play the melody in the slow movement) and the accompaniment to the two horns is given to violins and not to oboes as in the Brandenburg version.

In its early form it was, as I have pointed out, a piece of concerted music for orchestras; there was no suggestion of its being a concerto grosso and it is in this form that it constitutes the Introduction to Cantata No. 52, 'Falsche Welt, dir trau' ich nicht', also dated 1730.

Spitta, Volume 2, page 132, says: 'Appended to the Concerto

(No. 1) are a Minuet diversified by a Polacca and two Trios. These are fine music and a work of genius, but have nothing to do with the true concerto. Dance-forms were much in favour, as has been said, even in orchestral concerti, although they were in entire opposition to the ideal of the form. This is the only instance of Bach having made a concession to the taste of the time; and, as the dances can be separated from the rest of the work, if desired, they hardly impare its beauty'.

The $\frac{6}{8}$ Allegro which is now the third movement, and the Polonaise separating the two Trios, were added, I believe, at the time when Bach was making a fair copy of his own earlier MS to send to the Duke of Brandenburg. The style of the $\frac{6}{8}$ movement is unlike the remainder of the work and proves it to be a later addition.

This new movement appears again in the secular Cantata No. 207, 'Vereinigte Zwietracht der wechselnden Saiten' which is usually dated 1726. In it the two horn parts are given to three trumpets and the whole movement is transposed down into D.

Let us now return to our first movement.

Group 1 (corni), announces itself with traditional fanfares and is quite insistent on its ceremonial nature. The fanfares occur seven times during the movement*. (See Ex. 18.).

Group 2 (oboes), has a short chordal passage not unlike a slow, harmonized trill which appears no less than sixteen times. (See bars 1, 8, 9, 29, etc and Ex. 22.).

Group 3 (strings), provides a theme (bar 1) built on a simple chord followed by a few scale-wise notes. It is, of course, a variant of the horn fanfares. (Ex. 23.).

Bach's genius in adapting or re-shaping phrases, purely as music, is very evident even at this comparatively early stage in his career, but he has not yet learned to vary his writing instrumentally. In this work and in Concerto No. 2 all the solo or concertante instruments play the same music regardless of whether it suits them or not.

The only concession the composer makes—and it is one which the natural harmonic law forces upon him—is that he varies the pitch of passages to be played by corni or trumpets in such a way that he is able to employ the upper harmonics when melodic, as opposed to purely arpeggio, passages are required.

---

* We are greatly indebted to Mr Eric Halfpenny for his work in connection with these horn calls and fanfares.

Examples of the re-shaping just mentioned appear from bar six onwards; reference to the score shows that:

1. in bars 6 and 19 the oboes play a variant of the string theme
2. which is repeated immediately by the strings in bar 7
3. the extended semiquaver section of the theme is then dovetailed onto the chordal opening of the strings—(bars 8–10)
4. (bars 13–15) the oboes now combine their slow (semiquaver) trill with the string theme and, at the same time (bars 13 and 15), first the corni and then the strings take over the trills from the oboes and actually combine with them in bar 14.

Bach has a great liking for imitative passages. A typical one between corni and oboes occurs at bar 40 (it was noted on page 48). A similar passage, but between horns and strings, appears later at bar 69 (see also page 49).

In the final bars of the work each group reverts to its own special identification marks.

An interesting twist to an experiment occurs in bar 6. While the oboes are trying a variant of the strings' passage the bassoon, forsaking the continuo line for a moment, is allowed a solo bar. It consists of the 1st oboe's semiquaver passage (that is, the 2nd half of its bar) which is followed by the 2nd oboe's opening quavers—the whole passage being transposed a tone lower than the respective notes on the oboes.

Second Movement (Adagio).

This movement provides the only hint of sadness in the whole work. It consists, in the main, of a duet between the 1st oboe and the violino piccolo with comments on the thematic material from the cello, violone and bassoon. The horns are silent throughout.

In the original version, which had no part for piccolo violino, all the first violins played the melody now allotted to the solo instrument.

The movement opens with a lovely, serene, four-bar melody on the oboe which is accompanied by detached chords on the other two oboes and repeated quavers in the strings.

The solo violin enters at bar 5 and plays the oboe melody a fourth higher (a typical piece of Bach's writing).

The bass instruments make their first comment on the oboe theme at bar 9 when accompanied by swaying chords alternating between oboes and upper strings. Listeners should notice the clash between the A-flat in the bass and the C, F-sharp, A, chord on the fourth quaver of bar 9. This effect was introduced by Bach when the piccolo violino part was added. The original version, and another made in 1730, has A-natural in the bass line. This second version, although discordant, certainly gives a more shapely line to the bass melody.

At bar 12 the duet becomes a canon at one beat's distance. Particular attention should be paid to bars 14–17. Notice how the demisemiquaver 1st beat of the oboe (bar 14) becomes two groups of semiquavers (2nd and 3rd beats) in the violin. The two instruments are in step again for the 2nd and 3rd beats of bar 15, then, in bar 16, the violin repeats most of the oboe line of bar 15 a fourth higher, so changing the unison canon at one beat's distance to a canon a fourth apart and at one bar's distance.

Bars 20–23 repeat the bass version of the theme a tone higher than before and with the string and oboe chords reversed as regards their position in the bar. The clash of tonality is now between a B-flat in the basses and the chord D, G-sharp, B-natural, on the oboes (4th quaver of bar 20).

The canon reappears in bar 31 but with the piccolo violin leading. Similar changes of interval and distance are made as in the first statement.

Bar 31 brings the bass figure for the third time. On this occasion the clash is between an E-flat in the lower instruments and an E-natural in the 1st violins.

The movement is ushered towards its close by a quasi-cadenza passage on the 1st oboe over a held diminished-7th chord on C-sharp. A four-bar codetta brings the movement to an end on the dominant chord of A. The 2nd, 3rd and 4th bars from the end are particularly interesting. Notice how the continuo instruments play on the 1st beat; the oboes have a chord on the 2nd beat and the strings on the 3rd—all joining together for the final chord of A major. The effect of the widely differing chords and instrumental sonorities is mysterious and quite beautiful.

Third Movement. *Allegro*

It is probable that this movement was written in about 1720; the year during which Bach gave the solo violin Sonatas and Partitas to the world. The treble- and quadruple-stopping problems in the piccolo violin part of this Allegro are closely akin to similar passages in the solo works and it is logical to assume that Bach's mind was busily employed in solving them and others connected with solo string writing at that time.

The violin writing is extremely difficult—difficult enough when played on a piccolo violin—almost impossible on a normal sized and tuned instrument.

The two horns, having been rested during the slow movement, are given plenty to do now. We have discussed the horn versus trumpet problem earlier on in the book; if it is a fact that Bach intended the parts to be played by instruments of normal horn pitch, and that Leopold's two trumpeters did not play a horn-type instrument so that Bach was forced to await a visit from travelling horn virtuosi for a performance, then one gets the impression that the composer took good care to make the visitors' visit worthwhile and gave them every opportunity of proving their virtuosity!

The material from which the movement is formed is relatively simple. It consists of

a) three or four quavers followed by groups of four or six semi-quavers. (Bars 1, 2 and 3).
b) six semiquavers followed by three quavers. (Bars 8, 9 and 10).
c) an extended semiquaver passage with an attractive cross rhythm. (See Ex. 33).
d) quieter interludes. (Bars 53 and 74).

Oboes and strings lead off together with (a) repeating it a little later (bar 8) against the horns playing (b). (See Ex. 27).

Bar 12 and onwards introduces the first of the cross-rhythm passages (c) on 1st oboes and 1st violins. Although the passage is written in $\frac{6}{8}$ it is almost inevitable that it will sound as though in $\frac{3}{4}$ and I feel that this fact should be stressed and the necessary cross accents inserted in performance:

Ex 33. 1st. Oboe & 1st. Violin.

The piccolo violin makes his first solo appearance in bar 17 with a four-bar phrase based on the movement's initial passage. Some extremely unpleasant (from the player's point of view, that is) chords (see Ex. 14) appear in bar 25 and onwards and in bars 30–35 he is joined by the 1st horn in a duet consisting of a sequential passage of semiquavers in the one instrument against quavers in the other. (See Ex. 26).

Problems of balance, etc. in connection with this section were discussed in an earlier chapter (page 46).

The first interlude, a duet between 1st oboe and piccolo violin, is introduced at bar 53. This is the first point of repose in the movement and it could, I feel, be taken at a slightly slower speed than the rest of the movement. The slackening need not be obvious but the passage should produce a calmer mood.

The two horns have one of their fantastically difficult passages between bars 60 and 74. In the latter bar the piccolo violin and 1st ripieno violins re-introduce a quiet interlude similar to that which appeared at bar 53.

It is of interest to compare the music given to the solo violin in this movement—especially in the two interludes—with that allotted to the sopranos in Cantata No. 207 (Vereinigte Zwietracht der wechselnden Saiten), the second movement ('Coro') of which makes use of the Brandenburg Concerto material.

Ex. 34 (a) gives the violin passage and (b) the chorus sopranos' version:

A ritenuto begins in bar 80 and leads to a bar and a half of Adagio which is, in fact, a short cadenza for the solo violin. Some conductors seem to rush into the Adagio with no previous rit. or rall. I am convinced that this is wrong so far as this work is concerned. A fermata does not necessarily mean a stop with a sudden jolt as though all brakes had been applied in a crisis but a gradual slowing down as, for instance, when a red traffic light has been seen in good time.

The phrase (a) actually written for the solo violin in this Adagio is a little bald and angular and I am of the opinion that discreet ornamentation may be added somewhat as follows: (b) (See, also, Part III—page 121).

And here is the vocal version of this passage:

After the cadenza the piccolo violin leads the orchestra in a restatement of the original material and the movement is terminated at bar 124.

A normal three-movement concerto would end here but Bach adds a group of dance movements as follows:

Menuetto, Trio I, Menuetto again, Polacca (added at the same time as the ⅜ Allegro), Menuetto yet again, Trio II and the Menuetto repeated for the fourth time. The Menuetto consists of the customary two sections with wind and strings doubled throughout. There is a canon at one bar's distance between the top (melody) line and the bass, which causes a slight discord on the 2nd beats of bars two and three.

The horns have a relatively quiet time and are used, apart from a little flourish at the end of the movement, purely as a rhythm section—in fact—excluding the four closing bars—their parts could be played equally well on three tympani.

Trio I

This movement is for two oboes and bassoon only. It is a cheerful little piece of two unequal sections—the second being twice the length of the first.

Polacca

Strings only provide this movement and, as the solo violin is instructed by the composer to remain silent, it is, in effect, an opportunity for the ripieno or accompanying instruments to show their mettle—all the soloists being rested. The movement is quiet, smooth and peaceful apart from one small outburst.

Trio II

In the version we are discussing here this movement is a duet for two horns accompanied by the three oboes in unison. The earlier or original gave the accompaniment to the violins and I cannot help feeling that the effect would be better than in Bach's second thoughts. Three oboes can sound remarkably like ducks quacking unless the players (and the conductor) are extremely careful!

Note that in bars 3, 5 and 6 accompaniment and melody have the same notes. This, perhaps, provides good grounds for suggesting that the horns or melody line should sound an octave higher. This does occur in the arrangement of the movement which appears in Cantata No. 207 of 1726 where the original horn parts are given to trumpets and the accompaniment to strings in addition to oboes: (See, also, Ex. 28).

CHAPTER II

BRANDENBURG CONCERTO
No. 2

(Written in 1719)

TRUMPET

My remarks concerning the notes of the harmonic series on the horn (page 35) apply equally well to the trumpet bearing in mind that an instrument of half the length of the horn (i.e. approximately six feet long) will produce notes sounding an octave higher:

Ex.38.

It was customary to divide this wide compass between three players when using the instrument orchestrally. The top player covered from the sixth harmonic upwards and, according to Nicholas Comyn Gatty in 'Grove' (1928 edition) used a very fine bore instrument known as 'clarino' and having a very shallow mouthpiece; the second player played harmonics four to eight inclusive on a slightly wider bored instrument called 'tromba', and the lowest played harmonics one to five using an even wider bore and a deeper cup. His instrument was known as 'principale'. It is generally agreed now that the terms 'clarino', 'tromba' and 'principale' refer to specific registers, i.e. the 'clarino' register is the 3rd and 4th octave of the trumpet's compass and not a particular type of instrument. It is, of course, quite possible that the 1st trumpeter—who, naturally, played mostly in the clarino register—would use a shallower cupped mouthpiece than his colleagues in order to obtain the maximum assistance in the production of the high notes.

Bach, certainly, does not always appear to observe the distinctions mentioned by Gatty, see, for example, Cantata No. 31, 'Der Himmel lacht', where the three trumpets in unison play:

If Gatty is correct then Bach's 1st trumpeter would have to change from a 'clarino' to a 'tromba' or even a 'principale' or else play only the two highest notes of the passage!

Bach usually refers to the instrument as 'tromba' regardless of pitch, compass or tessitura. In only three instances does he refer to 'clarino' and only once to 'principale'. Also he expected his 1st player to be able to cover practically the entire compass of the instrument. Concerto No. 2 contains these notes:

This part used to be considered almost unplayable as it stands and various arrangements, e.g. the well-known one by Felix Mottl, which drops some of the high passages down an octave, have been made. Such famous players as Ernest Hall, the late Herbert Barr and George Eskdale and the younger players of the present day—Harold Jackson, Denis Clift, David Mason, etc.—have proved that this is not so and we are able to hear the work in all its glory. In spite of the great abilities of the players mentioned certain visiting conductors have substituted other instruments. Toscanini, for example, used an E-flat clarinet in 1938 and Enesco a sopranino saxophone in 1950.

The painting of Reiche by Hausmann depicts the player as holding a small, closely curled trumpet in his right hand and a piece of music in his left. The instrument has been measured as accurately as possible and was thought to be in D and fitted with a small 'C' crook. The music is as follows and covers from the fourth to the sixteenth harmonics. It would sound as written if played on a C instrument:

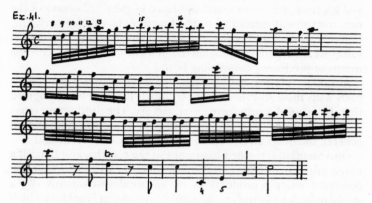

Ex. 41.

One can assume that a conscientious painter would be careful to depict the correct number of curls in an instrument but one cannot expect him to have his measurements absolutely exact and it is possible that the instrument is in F and carries an E-flat crook. In this case Concerto No. 2 would fit it perfectly and be quite playable on the instrument without the crook, i.e. in its basic key of F.

Recently experiments have been carried out by Steinkopf and Finke, the German wind instrument makers, and Walter Holy the 1st trumpeter of the Capella Coloniensis attached to Cologne Radio. The results of these experiments force us to change many of our pet theories regarding Bach's trumpets.

About seven years ago Cologne Radio decided to form an orchestra for the purpose of performing old music on old instruments. One of the first necessities was to search in German and other museums for wind instruments in excellent states of preservation which could be played or copied. Splendid copies were built but, in spite of many trials, all attempts to revive the old art of clarino playing on them seemed condemned to failure. The copies were, like the originals, about 7 feet 6 inches in length. In the fourth octave, where the notes are chromatic, the harmonics are so close together that the players found themselves constantly overblowing or breaking on to the next note. As early as the nineteenth century these difficulties had been overcome by the construction of instruments of half the length of the old. These short instruments were, of course, pitched an octave higher than the old natural trumpets. In this way the trumpet parts of Bach and his contemporaries could be played in the third octave of the new instrument instead of in the fourth octave as formerly. As, however, the natural notes lie at intervals of thirds in this octave, valves were invented to provide the new (short) trumpet with the means of producing the missing notes.

Although players could attain amazing accuracy in clarino parts with these so-called 'Bach' trumpets it was generally agreed that the musical results were unsatisfactory. The third octave is too strong and unyielding; the top is strident and unmetallic and, in general, the notes do not blend with the rest of the orchestra.

Otto Steinkopf, the first bassoonist of the Capella, and himself a noted instrument maker, was commissioned by Cologne Radio to construct exact reproductions of historical instruments. By a stroke of luck he found an old natural trumpet in Frankfurt which had a circular hole of the size of a pinhead in the tubing. This hole appeared to have been drilled and did not seem to be due to wear or corrosion. Soon after Steinkopf's discovery an English musical magazine carried an article on historical musical instruments in which was described an old trumpet with two similar perforations. Steinkopf made many experiments and calculations in an attempt to solve the mystery of these holes. Finally he came to the conclusion that their presence was not accidental but deliberate and that they were placed at exact nodal points for a purpose. He discovered that if one hole was left uncovered it was impossible to produce all the natural harmonics but if, however, both were covered then all the natural notes were readily playable. By the help of these holes it was possible to play in the clarino register with precision, the danger of overblowing on to an adjacent note had been removed.

The fact that these holes have to be bored at exact nodal points proves that the curl near the mouthpiece of Reiche's trumpet is not a crook for if a crook were fitted to an instrument carrying these holes they would automatically become in the wrong place relative to the now lengthened instrument and so render the 11th and 13th harmonics either even more out of tune than usual or make it impossible to produce tham at all.

I mentioned the 11th and 13th harmonics on page 35 when discussing the Jagdhorn. Those familiar with the laws of acoustics will remember that the 11th harmonic which occurs in the fourth octave is sharp and the 13th is flat. Steinkopf experimented still further and decided to drill yet a third hole in the trumpet tube. This hole, when uncovered, had the effect of raising the pitch of the trumpet by a fourth. Thus the harmonic series was raised and the note produced by the 11th harmonic in the original key was now given by the 8th harmonic and the original 13th by the new 10th. Therefore no intonation difficulties now existed.

The three holes have to be manipulated by the 1st and 3rd fingers and thumb of the player's right hand. Obviously he cannot support the instrument in the same hand. It must, therefore, be held by the left hand practically horizontally—almost, in fact, in a position similar to the corno da caccia. Terry's supposition that the bell was directed upwards is wrong.

The instruments made by Finke and based on Hausmann's picture and known contemporary examples of trumpets are cylindrical in bore. As horns are conical in bore the new instruments are, therefore, true trumpets and not small horns or Jagdhorns as suggested by Terry, who, in a letter to Ernest Hall dated March 27, 1931 says: 'The Reiche horn is a Jagdhorn (Cor da caccia). I gather that the bell was always upwards in that period'.

In the section on the horn, I mentioned that some scholars feel the horn parts in Concerto No. 1 should sound an octave higher than as usually played. On the other hand another musicologist claims that the trumpet part in Concerto No. 2 should sound an octave lower than usual on the grounds that there is a trumpet (?) in the Berlin Museum which sounds at the same pitch as a horn in F! He does not, however, say whether the F horn he had in mind was a horn in alt or at the usual twelve foot pitch.

Readers who are experienced concert goers and familiar with modern orchestral instruments will, perhaps, wonder at my references to the length of the trumpet. Let me say straight away

E

that the invention and introduction of the valve system enabled instrument makers to shorten the main or basic length of the instrument by fifty per cent. As I mentioned on page 64 valves bridge the gap between the second and third harmonics so that, in effect, the second harmonic acts as the fundamental, enabling the maker to dispense with that length of tubing required formerly to produce the real fundamental and first harmonic.

May I explain, quite briefly, the workings of the valve system for the benefit of those who are not completely familiar with modern brass instruments. The valves are three in number (we are referring to the trumpet only—other brass instruments may have more than three) numbered first, second and third counting from the mouthpiece end of the instrument, i.e. the first valve is the one nearest to the player's lip. Their depression brings into use additional and scientifically calculated lengths of tubing. The second valve lowers the pitch of a note by one semitone, the first valve by a tone, the first and second combined or the third alone by a tone and a half (or minor third), the second and third together by two tones or a major third, the first and third together by two and a half tones or perfect fourth and all three valves together lower the note by three tones or an augmented fourth. In this way the gap is bridged. Ex. 43 shows the valve bridge between harmonics 3 and 2.

The historical accuracy of Steinkopf's deductions was confirmed by the discovery of two old posthorns bearing similar 'transposition' holes. These instruments were found in the house of Bernoulli, the Swiss collector of instruments, by Helmut Finke the instrument maker who had been engaged to build the reproductions of natural trumpets.

On page 65 I said that Finke's instruments are based on Hausmann's picture. They are, in fact, very similar to the trumpet held by Gottfried Reiche and include the small curl mistaken in the past for a crook. They are soft in timbre and dynamic, beautifully in tune and blend perfectly with the other instrumental groups of the orchestra. One realises after hearing them that Bach knew perfectly well what he was doing when he added three high trumpets to his scores.

RECORDER

Bach writes Concerto No. 2 for 'Fiauto'

Bach writes Concerto No. 4 for 'due Fiauti d'Echo'

Bach writes Concerto No. 5 for 'une Traversiere'

In his day 'Blockflöte', 'Flöte', 'Flute', 'Flûte à bec', 'Flauto' (or 'Fiauto'), 'Flûte douce' or 'Flauto d'eco (or Echo)' meant 'Recorder'.

'Flûte d'Allemagne', 'Flûte allemande', 'Flauto traverso', 'Traversa', 'Flûte traversière', 'Traversflöte', 'Querflöte' meant the flute as we know it today, therefore Nos. 2 and 4 should be played on the Recorder and only No. 5 on the Flute.

Recorders were made in different sizes and keys. Concerto No. 2 requires these notes:

i.e. the normal range of a treble recorder in F. Chromatic from

Ex.45.

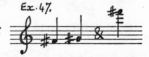

with the addition of the low F and G and the

high G. Note that Bach writes for it in the French treble clef, i.e. as a transposing instrument sounding a third higher than written. The 'French treble clef' used when writing for recorders and the piccolo violin is a G clef but has the curl of the clef sign on the

Ex. 46.

bottom line of the stave—thus: ⟨stave⟩ The stave lines are,

therefore, G, B, D, F, A.

Ex.47.

Concerto No. 4, in addition, calls for ⟨stave⟩

and poses special problems which will be considered when that work is discussed.

ANALYSIS

Concerto No. 2 in F à

1 Tromba ⎫
1 Flauto ⎪
1 Hautbois ⎬ Concertato
1 Violino ⎪

2 Violini ⎫
1 Viola é Violone ⎬ Ripieno

Col Cello è Basso per il Cembalo

This concerto, written in or about 1719, has the normal three movements—Allegro, Andante and Allegro Assai. It is a highly complicated work and it will be necessary to index the themes so that one may trace the wonderful and intricate jugglings to which they are submitted.

Theme I, bars 1 and 2—top voices:

Theme II, bars 1 and 2—basses:

Theme III, bars 5 and 6—top voices:

Theme IV, bars 7 and 8—top voices:

Theme V, bars 9 and 10—the main concerto theme:

Theme VI, bars 33 to 35—trumpet and oboes:

It is interesting to note that Bach allots the lowest line of the ripieno group to the violone or bass gamba, i.e. an instrument of sixteen foot pitch, leaving the cello, with its eight foot pitch, to combine with the harpsichord as continuo and to fill in the space between the viola and sixteen foot bass line.

First Movement (Allegro).

The work opens with an eight-bar tutti in which the recorder (flauto), oboe, solo violin and 1st orchestral violins play in unison. The trumpet (apart from a high trill in bars 3 and 4) combines with the viola in providing the necessary harmonic filling and the basses present a semiquaver figure (theme II). The composer makes good use of the first two bars of this figure later on.

The tutti ends at the half-bar and a short scale leads straight into the first statement, by the solo violin, of the concerto theme proper (V).

This is repeated two bars later by the oboe. Now follows the first change to which the bass semiquavers (theme II) are submitted. They appear in the trumpet (bars 15 and 16) *above* theme I on recorder, oboe and violins and with the trumpet notes of the first two bars of the movement constituting the bass line. The composer has, therefore, turned his bass line into a solo theme and used a former harmonic filling as a good, solid, bass.

The recorder now presents the concerto theme (V) (bars 17 and 18) and the trumpet, after repeating the bass theme (II), plays a new version of the concerto theme (bars 21 and 22). Bars 3 and 4 of the opening tutti, (now in the key of C), lead to a repeat of theme III on oboe and violins and, when joined later by the recorder, of theme IV.

Bach was, apparently, not quite satisfied with the trumpet's version of the concerto theme and so, in bars 29 and 30, permits him a restatement in a form more closely resembling the original.

The violins repeat theme I while the recorder plays theme II in thirds with the basses. After three bars, however, the recorder is allowed to scamper up to the extreme top of his instrument (bar 35).

Bar 32 introduces what, for convenience, we might consider as a new theme (labelled VI), but which is, in fact, an imitative passage derived from the last half-bar of theme I. It makes a pleasant little canonic duet between trumpet and oboe.

Themes III and IV of the tutti are now repeated and lead to restatements of:

a) theme I in D minor (on the trumpet) (bars 40 and 41)
b) theme II on oboe and solo violin (same bars) and, at the same time,
c) theme II (inverted) played by the recorder.

After these two bars trumpet and recorder change parts then the recorder reverts to theme II (bars 44 and 45) while the oboe takes over theme I. Two bars later (bars 46 and 47), the recorder plays theme I, the solo violin plays an inversion of theme II, while the basses play their own theme as in the first bars.

An imitative passage based on theme III is introduced at bar 50 and this section of the movement ends in B-flat with theme IV. This cadence is followed by four statements of the concerto theme (V) by recorder, solo violin, oboe and, finally, trumpet.

Bar 68 brings back theme I in C minor. This is followed by a passage similar to that introduced in bar 50, which leads on to another version of the trumpet-oboe duet (theme VI) and a G minor passage for trumpet taking him up to high G.

The combination of themes I and II introduced in bar 40 is repeated in G minor at bar 84 with theme I on the oboe, theme II on the recorder and II (inverted) on the trumpet.

At bar 86 the solo violin adds to theme I by inserting a semiquaver D between the first E and the C-sharp. This leads to a half-bar canonic treatment of theme I between trumpet and basses in D minor while recorder, oboe and solo violin accompany with a variant of theme II.

A little later, at bar 94, the canon, now in A minor, is between recorder and violin playing in sixths and trumpet and oboe also in sixths. There is, therefore, a double canon, the one between violin and oboe and the other, sounding simultaneously, between recorder and trumpet.

Theme (or sub-theme), VI returns in bar 95, this time between

recorder and solo violin. It leads to theme III in the bass with
theme IV on oboe and violins and a full close in A minor. A
wonderful tutti restatement of theme I in F leads quite naturally
out of the cadence. The trumpet, through its inability to sound
a B-flat in the correct register, has to vary the theme slightly. A
few bars of theme III treated as in bars 50–58 and 72–76 ushers in a
tutti statement of theme III and IV bringing the movement to a
triumphant close in its home key.

I pointed out, in connection with Concerto No. 1, that, at this
stage in his career, Bach was contented to make only such altera-
tions to his themes (in order to fit them to different instruments)
as the actual technical capabilities of the instruments demanded.
This applies equally to this work. See, for example, how the
trumpet is forced to change the shape of the concerto theme (V)
in bars 21 and 22 as compared with the normal version in a different
key in bars 29 and 30. It should be remembered that the low C-sharp
was a risky note for Bach's oboist. Notice how the composer
overcomes this difficulty by changing the C-sharp to an E in the
oboe part in bars 40 and 41, and how the trumpet has to play
E-flat, E-flat, C, instead of E-flat, D, C, in bar 55. One must realise
that these changes were not dictated by musical considerations
but purely by the technical or mechanical short-comings of the
instruments concerned.

Second Movement (Andante).

The trumpet is rested in this movement and the accompaniment
to the recorder, oboe and solo violin is provided by cello and
harpsichord only.

The thematic material is simple in that there are only two
basic themes. The first of these is announced by violin, oboe and
recorder. The second, to which further reference will be made
later, is, perhaps, not a theme in its own right but a portion of
No. 1. I have, however, shown it as theme II in Ex. 54.

Theme I is varied—first by the recorder (bar 8); then by the oboe at bar 16 and, finally a third version is allotted to the violin in bar 24 and repeated immediately by the recorder, but before the recorder has reached the end of its version the oboe restates the basic themes I and II.

At bar 33 Bach shows what can be done by a master with so simple a germ of a theme as a falling tone or semitone:

This is introduced by the oboe again at bar 43 and is coupled with the variant which appeared in bar 24. Suggestions or reminders of theme I from violin, oboe and recorder bring this lovely movement peacefully and quietly to a close on a chord of D major.

Third Movement (Allegro Assai).

This movement is as youthfully vigorous as the Andante was calm and soothing. There are six recognisable themes apart from flowing semiquaver passages which serve as fillings-in or accompaniment. It will, I feel, be advisable to introduce and number them in advance of their appearances during the course of the movement.

Theme I is announced by the trumpet:

Theme II is in the continuo:

Theme III (played by the oboe) appears in bar 13:

Theme IV—a sequential passage of semiquavers divided between recorder and violin is introduced at bar 34:

Theme V—a passage in thirds—is announced at its first appearance in bar 47 by trumpet and violin:

Theme VI accompanies V and is given to the oboe:

The two themes are extremely alike—were we dealing with stamps instead of music we would say that VI was a 'variety' of V having had certain features displaced in printing. As it is we can just note that in V the pair of semiquavers falls on the 4th quaver of the bar whereas in VI it comes on the 2nd quaver.

The movement opens with theme I played by the trumpet and accompanied by theme II in the continuo. Bach gives trills to various notes of theme I during its different appearances. Just for interest I have added them all to the themes as shown in Ex. 56.

Theme I is taken over by the oboe at bar 7 and leads, at bar 13, to theme III (also played by the oboe). It is of a fugal nature—the oboe entry being followed two bars later by the trumpet (see Ex.57).

Theme I—which is, in fact, the main concerto theme—is now (bar 21) repeated by the solo violin but with the original continuo accompaniment (theme II) played a sixth above it by the trumpet.

The recorder is the last member of the concertante group to announce theme I (bar 27) and in this appearance it is accompanied by theme II but played a third below by the oboe.

The trumpet, still playing theme I and accompanied by theme II —on the solo violin this time—enters at bar 41. This short passage serves to introduce those themes (V and VI) which have yet to be announced.

In bar 57 the violin plays theme I accompanied by II played a sixth above by the recorder. Later, in bar 66, the oboe is responsible for theme I with II a tenth below on the violin. Further on still (bar 72), the basses have theme I with the accompanying theme II played two octaves and a third above them by the recorder.

This leads to an interesting development commencing at bar 79. Here, the recorder, playing at the extreme top of his instrument, is in sixths with the trumpet in a combined version of theme V. Theme VI is in the basses and oboe and violin, also in sixths, have a sequential semiquaver figure which serves to fill in the space between V and VI.

Now, commencing at bar 87, the four concertante instruments in turn re-introduce theme III. Bar 97 brings back themes V and VI, V on basses and oboe (two octaves and a third apart) and VI in the trumpet.

The oboe has the main theme (I) in bar 107 and is accompanied by theme II on the trumpet. This pair of themes is taken over by recorder and oboe in bar 113 and by basses and recorder in bar 119.

Bar 126 recalls the development introduced in bar 79. On this occasion violin and oboe (in thirds) play theme V with recorder (again at the top of his range) supplying the complementary theme VI, while the semiquaver passage is transferred to basses and trumpet.

Finally, at bar 136, the trumpet, who was allowed to open the movement, is given the last word and plays theme I accompanied by II on the violins.

In this movement especially Bach breaks right away from the 'Gemeinschafts-spielmusik' style of Concerto No. 1. This is real Concerto-grosso writing—almost all the interest is in the concertante group and the ripieno is reduced to a merely, very slight, accompanying role.

CHAPTER III

BRANDENBURG CONCERTO
No. 3 in G
(Written about 1718 or 1719)
à

tre violini ⎫
tre viole è ⎬ concertato
tre violoncelli ⎭
col Basso per il Cembalo

ANALYSIS

The concerto opens with an eight-bar, three-part, tutti. The three
violins are in unison, the three violas are also in unison and the
three cellos join with the continuo. The thematic material set out
in this tutti is of great importance as almost the whole first movement grows out of it. Notice especially the little group marked 'A'
in the first bar, also in the second bar of the cello part and the
fourth bar of the viola line—it is present, either wholly or in part,
in nearly every bar of the movement.

Theme I:

Theme II:

The unison passage in bars 7 and 8 produces a wonderfully strong effect after the busy semiquavers for the violins in bars 5 and 6.

Immediately after the opening tutti first the divided violins and then the violas show the general pattern Bach is to evolve from group A. Also in bars 37, 38 and 39 where he takes the group from the bottom of the ensemble to the top and down again. Another fine, three-part, passage appears at bar 12.

Just prior to this (bars 10 and 11) the three violins have introduced an imitative figure—a device which is used extensively throughout the movement and by the different instrumental groups.

Here are bars 10 and 11 for the violins:

They are repeated by the violas in bars 17 and 18 and in bars 62 and 63 by cellos.

An interesting effect commences in bar 23. It is a canon at the octave at one bar's distance (in D) between 1st violin and 1st viola followed immediately by a similar canon, but now in G, between the 2nd violin and 2nd viola. Later, at bar 31, the three violins combine to present a similar idea in a chordal passage followed, again immediately, by the three violas. One imagines that Bach felt three cellos playing a chordal passage of the same type would sound extremely gruff and unwieldy for, at bar 53, he allows his three cellos to play part of the theme in unison.

The chordal version of the theme, as opposed to the canonic form, is used several times during the course of the movement: e.g., bars 40/41 and 103/104 by violins, bars 101/102 by violas, bars 55/56 and 106/107 by cellos (in unison) and bars 105/106 by violas again but in unison this time. Notice how very easily and naturally all this has grown out of bars 2 and 3 of the opening tutti.

Let us return to bar 47, where we find the 1st violin launching a cadenza-like figure which also has been derived from bars 2 and 3. It is taken over immediately by the 2nd violin and, later (bar 66), by the 3rd violin. The 1st violin plays a very much extended version in bars 91 and onwards. This cadenza sub-theme is dropped for a time while the three violins and three violas develop the 'A' group (bars 97 onwards). After this development section all the strings return to the cadenza figure and it is allowed to run right through the ensemble. Notice that cellos, again, are in unison. This scheme is repeated between bars 107 and 118.

Once again we must go back a few bars to bar 78 and onwards. Here, first the 1st violin and then the 2nd, introduces the new theme (II), which is extremely reminiscent of the composer's violin concerto in E major, against the first bar-and-a-half of the opening tutti. Later, at bar 86, the 1st and 2nd violas have the opening theme against the 'E major' theme in 3rd violin and 3rd viola.

A well-known harpsichordist once told me that at a certain rehearsal he tried out part of the E major concerto, transposed into G, and found that some of it fitted quite well (see Ex. 62).

Finally, at bar 126, the opening eight-bar tutti returns but is extended by three bars. Bach inserts a short passage akin to that announced by the cellos in bar 37 into the second half of the seventh bar and by means of an extra half-bar of scales (bar 135) leads back into the original second half-bar. The final tutti is, therefore, one of eleven bars.

Notice the composer's superb disregard for mixed harmonies in bar 135:

On pages 42 and 53 we discussed the possibility of Concerto No. 1 having been a work of three movements in its original form and we saw how the introduction of the Allegro $\frac{6}{8}$ (the present third movement) changed the scheme of the work completely.

Bach's usual concerto form was three movements arranged quick, slow, quick and the other Brandenburgs adhere to this shape. No. 1, however, with its group of short dance movements as a Finale, is neither true concerto nor suite.

In No. 3 we are up against a different problem as now, in the great majority of performances, we are invited to believe that the work is in two movements connected by two cadential chords. Modern scholarship is, I think, beginning to accept the proposition that Bach intended the work to have a slow movement and that the two chords referred to are *its* cadence and not a mere link. The fact that, so far as we know, Bach omitted to commit the movement to paper suggests that, like Handel in somewhat similar circumstances, i.e. the organ concertos, he intended to play the movement himself as a solo. We know that he liked to play the viola in Leopold's orchestra whenever possible (see remarks on No. 5, page 99) and the technical difficulties of the first viola part in No. 3 would make his presence in the first desk extremely important. We are, therefore, faced with the picture of Bach playing 1st viola in the first and third movements and wandering over to the harpsichord to extemporise a solo slow movement. The two chords at the end of this movement each contain three notes for violas but in the first chord the 1st viola plays the same note as the 1st violin and in the second chord doubles the 3rd violin. In fact, therefore, and without resorting to double stopping, the chord is complete with only two violas.

Yehudi Menuhin, Thurston Dart and Geraint Jones have inserted suitable movements from violin and keyboard sonatas, etc. in their more recent performances.

The Menuhin Chamber Orchestra performed all six concertos at the Bath Festival in 1959. On this occasion Menuhin, together with the 1st viola and cello and harpsichord continuo played an arrangement of the Lento (E minor $\frac{6}{8}$) from Trio Sonata No. 6 (BWV 530). This is thought to have been written about 1720 or 1727.

Thurston Dart, both for his Oiseau-Lyre recordings and in a recent broadcast, included a movement from BWV 1021.

In one of the performances of the work given by the Geraint Jones Orchestra, Winifred Roberts (the leader of the orchestra) and Geraint Jones, also played the Largo from the Sonata for Violin and Figured Bass (BWV 1021) dating from about 1720. This is, of course, quite permissible but I prefer a solo harpsichord movement. Some years ago when working on a continuo for the complete work I transposed a section of the Toccata in F-sharp Minor into E Minor. It fitted very well and was about the correct length, (28 bars). I quote the opening and closing bars:

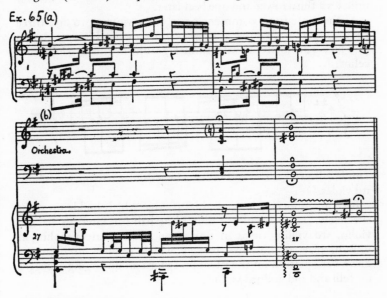

Ex. 65(a)

(b)

Orchestra.

Third Movement (Allegro).

This movement consists of 48 bars divided into two sections of unequal length, one of 12 and the other of 36 bars, each section being repeated. One notices immediately in it that Bach reduces the complexity of the writing very considerably by using the three groups in unison to a great extent—the three celli, for example, are in unison throughout. This, of course, is liable to make the movement sound rather bottom-heavy unless great attention is paid to internal balance.

This movement opens with the three violins enjoying one of Bach's familiar imitative passages:

Ex. 66

while the three violas (in unison) play a broken chord and scale passage which appears in many guises throughout the movement. Halfway through the 2nd bar the unison cellos take up the opening phrase and turn it into a sequential figure which the 1st violin imitates a third lower and one beat later.

At the same time, commencing in bar 3, violins two and three have a separate imitative passage of their own—the semiquavers of which run in sixths with similar groups in the 1st violin and cellos:

This is followed at the end of bar 6 by a similar passage for 1st and 3rd violas.

Bar 8 introduces a long chordal passage which builds up most effectively. The 1st violin, followed at half-bar intervals by 2nd violin, 3rd violin, violas in unison and (a bar later) violins in unison, play an imitative passage which resolves itself into a downward pattern on the 1st violin against an upsurging arpeggio on celli and 2nd and 3rd violins:

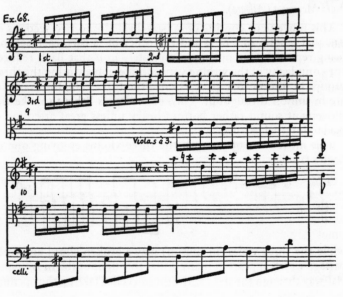

The 3rd bar of the second section introduces a new, cadenza-like, figure on the 1st violin:

which is repeated a third lower by the 1st viola in bars 35 and 36. This violin figure is followed by one of the sequential figures so beloved of Bach; first on violins and then on violas. Immediately afterwards, at bar 24, the three violins, followed by violas and then by violins again, repeat the chordal passage (transposed down a third) which concluded the first section (see Ex. 68). But, on this occasion, Bach deftly leads into a fresh phrase which violins and violas toss from one to the other:

At bar 32, violas launch the chordal figure which, with a slightly different ending, leads to the viola cadenza mentioned earlier on (see Ex. 69).

The music, which is full of high spirits and one of Bach's happiest and most exhilarating movements, continues on much the same lines until once again the violas introduce the chordal passage (Ex. 68). This time the composer allows the cadence to stand and the work ends with a triumphant flourish on a chord of G.

It is fascinating to speculate on the actual players who may have performed in this Concerto.

Spiess and Markus would, of course, have played first and second violin. Abel, who played violin in addition to gamba, would be required in the cello section and, therefore, not available as third violin. Bach himself would, no doubt, play first viola. Linigke, being a cellist, would, most probably, play first cello leaving Abel, a gambist, as second. This leaves us with third violin, second and third viola, third cello and bass positions to fill. Perhaps J. H. Freytag or Wurdig (flutes) played third violin.

81

F

Possibly J. Freytag played viola and, perhaps, Fischer, too, was a viola player. Also it would be nice to think that Leopold himself played third cello, unless Torlen the bassoonist played cello and Leopold provided the harpsichord continuo to the first and third movements.

Tovey (see his *Essays in Musical Analysis* page 190) is of the opinion that 'This work is a concerto grosso . . . but . . . a concerto in which there is no actual solo . . .'. I feel that if we hold to that opinion we must call the work a 'Concerto grossissimo' as there are nine instruments in the concertante group, none in the ripieno and but two providing the continuo. In actual fact what happens is that the nine soloists take it in turns to join up with each other in varying combinations and provide either a tutti or a ripieno accompaniment to whoever happens to be playing the solo part or parts at that particular moment.

Heinrich Besseler, on the other hand, regards Nos. 1 (in its original form) and 3 as being examples of what he calls 'Gemein-schafts-Spielmusik', that is 'music for mutual participation or possession or for the common interest'. Later works, Nos. 2 and 4 (and 1 in its revised version), were concerti grossi (Gruppen-konzerte). No. 5, rather a mixture, began life as a concerto grosso, became a solo keyboard concerto part way through the first movement, turned into pure chamber music in the second movement and reverted to concerto grosso status in the Finale.

No. 3, of course, should be played by single strings. The well-known modern practice of dividing all the available orchestral violins, violas and cellos into three sections and leaving probably six or eight basses to 'sustain' the continuo line cannot be deprecated too strongly. Just imagine the problems of balance a conductor of a good-sized orchestra creates for himself. Take an orchestra whose string strength is 16:14:12:10:8 and we find ten violins, four violos, three cellos (plus one odd man out) and eight basses to a part! In addition, as the cellos are in unison in the Finale and join forces with the basses, eighteen instruments would be grinding out the bass line. The movement would be so bottom-heavy as to sink!

CHAPTER IV

BRANDENBURG CONCERTO
No. 4 in G
(Written during the winter of 1719/20)

Concerto 4to à Violino Principale.
due Flauti d'Echo.
due Violini,
una Viola è Violone in Ripieno,
Violoncello è Continuo.

ANALYSIS

This work is unique among the Brandenburgs in that it could be
written for only one solo instrument, in which case it would be,
strictly speaking, a solo concerto and not a concerto grosso.
Spitta, however, in Volume 2, page 133, of his book on Bach, says:
'It (No. 4) is a concerto grosso in the manner of No. 2' (and, in a
footnote, goes on to say) 'W. Rust, in the B.G. edition, is wrong in
calling it a violin concerto. The word ripieno in the title applies
only to the violins since there are no flauti ripieni. Besides this, the
intention is clear from the work itself. Dehn, in the Peters edition,
gives it the right title'.

Certainly a tradition appears to have grown up over the years of
regarding it as a triple concerto for violin and two recorders.
Reference to the facsimile score shows that Bach himself described
it as in the heading to this chapter while the title page of the
Eulenburg (1928) edition of the miniature score refers to the work
as for:

Konzertierende Violine
mit Begleitung von
2 Flöten (Flûtes à bec), 2 Violinen, Viola, Violoncell und Continuo.

On the other hand the new Barenreiter edition of the complete
Brandenburgs (1956) brackets together Violino principale, Flauto
dolce I and Flauto dolce II as concertante, and the remaining

83

instruments as ripieno accompaniment. So, too, does the Broude Bros. edition prepared by Kurt Soldan. Other known editions or copies describe the work as follows:

1) A score in an unknown handwriting in the Amalien-Bibliothek.
   'Concerto Violino à Voc: 9.
   Violino Principale.
   Due Flauti d'Echo.
   Due Violini Viola Violone in Ripieno.
   Violoncello e Cembalo'.

2) An old score in an unknown handwriting in Westdeutschen Bibliothek Marburg.
   Concerto IVto a Violino principale,
   due Flauti d'Echo
   Due Violini, una Viola, Violoncello,
   Violone ripieno e Basso continuo'.

by the side of the word 'Violone' is 'ô Contrabasso' and by 'continuo' is 'sul Clavicembalo'. These amendments are in the (known) handwriting of Zelter.

3) In the same library a set of parts written by J. A. Patzig, they are enclosed in a cover bearing the inscription:
   'Concerto à tre:

   Violino ⎫
   Flauto Imo ⎬ principale
   Flauto 2do ⎭

   Violino 1mo ⎫
   Violino 2do ⎪
   Viola ⎬ ripieno
   Violoncello ⎪
   Contrabasso ⎭

da Giovanni Sebastiano Bach. No. 4 della Colezzione di sei Concerto Grossi'.

Notice that in his own score Bach puts full stops (.) after the words 'Principale' and 'd'Echo' and commas (,) after 'Violini' and 'Ripieno'. This may be his way of indicating that the first named instruments are concertante or, possibly, that a slip of his pen caused a dot instead of a comma to appear after 'd'Echo'.

Without any doubt whatsoever it will be agreed that the recorder parts are of great interest and importance as compared with parts written for the other (accompanying) instruments.

I mentioned on page 67 that Concerto No. 4 poses special problems relating to the recorders. Recorder No. 1 uses these notes (written in normal treble clef):

Ex. 71.

chromatic, that is, throughout the usual two-octaves range of a

recorder in G but omitting:

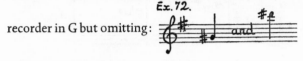

Ex. 72.

and

Recorder No. 2, however, adds these:

Ex. 73.

but omits

This downward range proves that Bach intended the second player to use a recorder in F and this proof is strengthened by the layout of certain passages in the first movement:

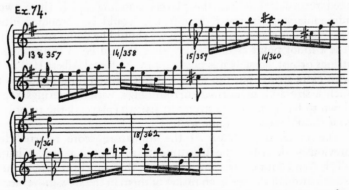

Ex. 74.

Notice the shape of this phrase; five consecutive notes in one bar which lead to a sixth at the beginning of the next. Observe that this is the top note of a broken chord. Now compare this phrase with the one which occurs in bars 47–52, 275–280 and 391–396 with particular attention to bars 49 and 50, 277 and 278 and 393 and 394:

Ex. 75.

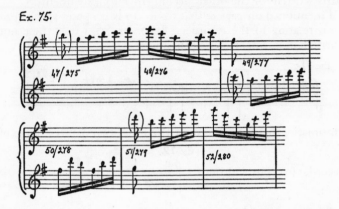

Obviously the phrase requires a top F-sharp in bars 50 and 278, but the substitution of the lower octave suggests that Bach knew the top note was extremely difficult to produce at speed or that the player at his disposal just could not get it at all.

Thurston Dart, in a performance given with Philomusica at the Royal Festival Hall, London, some years ago, used two flutes but had the players sitting in front of the strings. Basil Cameron, in the 1956 season of Promenade Concerts at the Royal Albert Hall, used recorders but had the players standing up. If these two admirable steps in the right direction could be combined into two recorder players sitting down we should be doing really well. It is a moot point as to whether they should be in front of the strings or not. Possibly it is necessary in the Royal Albert Hall and with extra strings but the work was not written for a building of such a size and, in normal surroundings, with the strings kept down to Bach's favourite strength: 3:3:2:1:1 (players), the recorder tone should stand out quite well.

The Eulenburg edition of the miniature score referred to previously describes the instruments as 'Flutes a bec'. 'Flauti d'Echo' and 'Flutes a bec' are, of course, the same instruments but examination of the use Bach makes of them in the slow movement of this concerto gives a possible reason why he preferred to call them 'Flauti d'Echo' on this occasion.

In his article, 'Bach's Flauti d'Echo', in the October 1960 volume of *Music and Letters,* Dart put forward some interesting theories. He suggests the possibility that Bach intended the recorder parts to be played on bird flageolets in G which would sound an octave higher than the written notes.

There are, I think, several points which can be made against this suggestion. The first, and possibly the most convincing, is the detail I have given of Bach's changing the layout of certain of his second recorder's passages in order to avoid the top F-sharp. This would be quite unnecessary on a G flageolet.

The second is that the flageolets are even quieter than recorders and Dart's comment that '. . . the gentle sounds of two treble recorders are quite inaudible . . .' would apply with even greater force to two flageolets—described by Dart as 'with an extremely soft tone'. Even the higher pitch of the latter instruments would not compensate for the fact that their power is only about half that of a sopranino recorder.

The third point, and I think, a valid one, is that Bach was a serious-minded man and unlikely to be influenced in any way by what Dart refers to as 'the fashion for the new-fangled flageolet'.

In the beginning of this chapter I described the concerto as possibly unique. Equally it is odd in the sense that practically all the interest in the first movement lies in the recorders. The solo violin has to content itself, most of the time, by playing in thirds, sixths and tenths with the recorders or else doubling the orchestral strings. It is not until the eighty-third bar is reached that it is allowed a real solo passage. In bars 39–40 and 383–384 it actually doubles the continuo line while the cello and violone are resting!

The third movement is marked 'Presto' but the Presto must not I feel, be taken too literally or the solo violin will be quite unable to play the repeated notes in his bar 103–119 passage as written (especially bars 106, 107, 114 and 115)—so, 'non troppo presto'!

Traces of a part for recorder may be detected in the facsimile score (bars 106–119).

Ex. 76.

These notes bear no resemblance to the solo violin part so it cannot be that Bach started to write for the latter instrument on the wrong stave and, in any case, the notes are not in Bach's handwriting. I wonder who added this passage and if he did so, perhaps, when the work was played at Cöthen, or whether someone needed a scrap of MS paper on which to jot down an idea and made use of the first blank stave he could find in the Brandenburg library?

First Movement

Theme I

Theme II

Theme III

The work opens with a broken chord on the 2nd recorder followed by four bars in thirds. At the seventh bar the same phrase is repeated, but with the recorders changing parts so that the thirds become sixths.

The thirteenth bar introduces one of Bach's favourite sequential imitative passages for the recorders with the solo violin playing (a) in thirds with the moving recorder and (b) doubling the orchestral first violins in alternate bars (Ex. 78).

Bars 23 and 29 restate Theme I and a new Theme (III) (Ex. 79) is announced by the recorders at bar 35. Note that the next phrase is a descending one:

Bar 57 brings back Theme I but bar 69 re-introduces Theme III—this time in an ascending version.

The solo violin has, so far, been occupied with passages based on Theme II. Chords tossed to and fro between strings and wind produce a delightful effect in bars 79 and 80.

When bar 83 is reached the soloist is allowed to demonstrate that he is present to play a concerto and launches Ex. 81:

This, and similar passages, last until bar 125 over an accompaniment which is so slight as to be practically non-existent. The recorders, however, interpose two bars of Theme I three times. (Bars 89/90, 103/104, 111/112).

Bar 125 brings back Theme II on the recorders followed by the same phrase repeated on orchestral violins. Then follow Theme I (bar 137) and III (bar 143) and the wind/string chords (bars 153–155) leading to an extended version of I (bar 185) which, in addition, gives the solo violin another opportunity to assert his independence. He launches a demi-semiquaver passage which carries him on to bar 209 when Theme I reappears once again. The soloist gives the impression of being angry with the recorders for their interruption and almost snatches this theme from them—going so far as to play the passage in sixths by himself (bar 217).

The wind/string chords return in bars 231–233 and in bar 235 a new passage with a canon at a quaver's distance appears in solo and orchestral violins. I have grouped the orchestral violins across the bar lines in this extract so that the sound pattern may be quite clear:

Ex. 82

The solo violin's concerto theme (Ex. 81) returns once more but is interrupted by the recorders. Bar 251 brings back the canonic passage (Ex. 82) on strings. Theme II reappears on strings in bar 263 and recorders at bar 267. This is followed by Theme III, also on recorders (271), and II at bar 275. Bar 311 sees the orchestral violins begin Theme II in sequence, recorders take it over for four bars and then hand it back to the violins who use it to lead back to Theme I (bar 323). Instead of this leading to its normal inversion Theme III is substituted (bar 329). The attractive device for wind/strings appears again and finally the main Theme I returns at bar 345.

The music now goes through the same sequence of phrases as in the opening tutti and the movement closes at bar 427 with the wind/string phrase which, from bar 423 onwards, provides a most effective and lighthearted coda.

Second Movement (Andante).

The first 24 bars of this movement could well serve to show why Bach made use of the term 'Flauti d'Echo' instead of any of the many other names under which recorders were known.

Ex. 83.

Recorders, solo and orchestral violins, play two bars forte followed by the same phrase repeated piano by recorders alone (the solo violin being used here solely to provide a few notes of accompaniment); later, bars 9–12, the phrases are reduced to one bar but the echo effect remains constant.

If this were not such a lovely and deeply felt movement one could, perhaps, imagine that Bach was playing a joke on his solo violinist for he permits the recorders to try their very hardest to prove that it is really their movement. Recorder No. 1 goes so far as to provide two little cadenzas at bars 29 and 31—the soloist having to be content to join up with the orchestral violins from bars 24–45 with the exception of four quavers in bar 32 and two in bar 33 where he is in thirds with the second recorder.

Finally the recorder is given a two-bar cadenza before the two closing chords.

Third Movement (Presto)

This movement, with its long opening tutti, lasting for 40 bars, is a mass of fugal entries.

Theme I, in the violas, bar 1:

Theme II, in the violas, bar 3:

Theme III, in the 2nd recorder, bar 47:

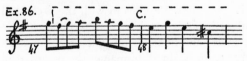

Theme IV, the solo violin's cadenza, bar 41:

The 2nd violin answers the viola entry at bar 5 which answer is repeated an octave higher by the recorder at bar 23.

The solo violin, still being treated rather shabbily, has to double the 1st (orchestral) violin until a cadence is reached at bar 40. Then, in bar 41, he launches a semi-cadenza (Ex. 87) which carries the music along to bar 63. This cadenza passage is accompanied only by the two recorders which announce the fugal subject A at two-bar intervals treating it almost canonically. At the fifth bar the 2nd recorder brings in the new theme, III (Ex. 86) which, lasting for six bars, is taken up five bars later by the 1st recorder.

At bar 63, 1st violins, followed by 2nd violins at bar 65 and violas at bar 67, introduce theme II treated canonically, while, at bar 67, cellos and violone announce theme I with its second section extended for twelve bars.

Bar 79 sees another statement of Theme I from the 1st and solo violins and, at bar 87, after a cadence in E minor, the solo violin restates his own cadenza theme (IV) accompanied first by cello and violone in minims and then by soft chords on the upper strings and recorders alternately.

The solo violin's part becomes really virtuosic from bar 100 to 120 with swirling semiquaver scales and broken chords across the strings against a very light string accompaniment. The orchestral strings join him with theme I in E minor at bar 127 which is followed by Theme II on recorders (bar 131) and I in the basses at bar 135.

At bar 152 the soloist adds a counterpoint to Theme I played in sixths by the recorders. He joins in with the orchestral strings at bar 175 and again adds his own counterpoint to the recorders playing Themes I and III at bar 179. The orchestra re-enters at bar 189 but in bar 193 he again accompanies the recorders in Themes I and III for ten bars.

Bach makes most effective use of a little three-note figure derived from the second part of Theme I between bars 219 and 224 where it is handed back and forth between recorders, 1st violin and viola. Once again the soloist is reduced to providing accompanying arpeggios and from bar 225 stays with the orchestral 1st violins to the end of the work. (Ex. 88).

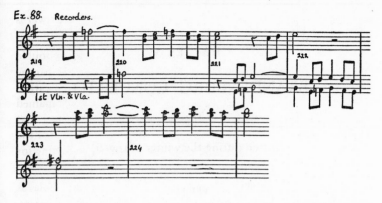

Ex. 88. Recorders.

Between bars 220 and 233 Bach introduces a staccatissimo sign (¹) over minims—this does not mean that the notes are to be played as short as possible nor that they must carry a heavy accent. This sign was used in Bach's day to denote an ordinary staccato—the notes which bear it in this instance should, therefore, be played as crochets separated by crochet rests.

We must return to bar 159 for a moment. Here we note a most interesting feature in that the harpsichord breaks away from the string bass. It will be remembered that the cello is the bass of the ripieno group in this concerto and the violone supports the continuo. In bars 159–174 inclusive the violone is silent, the cello becomes the 'base' of the whole orchestral edifice and the harpsichord provides a little variation of its own.

Something similar happens in the first movement (see bars 161, 163, 165–186 and 293–311), where the harpsichord bass is an ornamented version or variation of the cello line—or, if you wish—the cello line is a simplified version of the harpsichord bass.

This is, perhaps, the beginning of the harpsichord's independence —to be followed up and extended greatly in Brandenburg No. 5.

CHAPTER V

BRANDENBURG CONCERTO
No. 5

(Written during the winter of 1720/21)

FLUTE

The Modern Music-Master referred to on page 36, gives:

'As a gracefull posture, in playing on this Instrument, no less engages the Eyes of the beholders, than its agreeable Sound does their Ears; I shall therefore begin this Treatise, by describing one proper to use in playing thereon.

'Whether you Sit or Stand the Body must be erect, the head rather rais'd then inclin'd and somewhat turn'd to the left Shoulder, ye hands high, without raising the Elbows, or Shoulders, the left wrist bent inwards, and the left Arm close to the Body. If you play Standing, stand firm, with the left foot a little advanc'd, and rest the weight of your Body on the right leg, and all without any constraint, and observe never to make any motion with the Body, or head, as some do in beating Time.

'You need not think of placing your fingers at first, but only blow into the Flute, with all the holes open, till you are able to fill it and bring out a right tone, then place the fingers of the left hand in order, one after another and blow to each Note, till you are well assur'd of the truth of ye tone, ye put down ye fingers of ye right hand in like manner; you need not trouble yourself to fill the first Note, because it can't be done without stopping all the holes perfectly well, which is harder to do than one would imagine, and must be attained by practice only. When you have arrived at filling the Instrument, then proceed to learn your Scale'.

Johann Joachim Quantz gave fingering instructions for flute in his *Versuch einer Anweisung die Flöte traversiere zu spielen* of 1752.

The instrument in question was one with six finger holes and two right hand little finger keys, one for D-sharp and the other for

E-flat. Its compass was from:

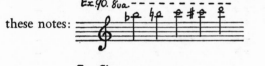

And the first edition of Volume VI of the French Encyclopaedia edited by Diderot in 1756 gives a scale of fingering which includes

these notes:

Two notes, each had no less than three

alternative fingerings in order to facilitate good intonation in passage work.

Quantz's first chart gives fingering for the diatonic scale of C only but all the missing notes are readily available, see second chart.

Chart I

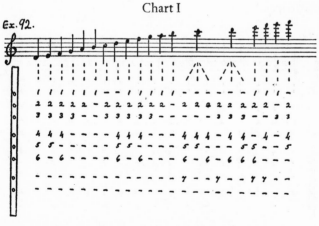

(7 = the E-flat key and 8 = the D-sharp key)

95

Chart II

Ex.93.

The writer of this article in *The Modern Music-Master* quoted above says:

'F in altissimo for the most part cannot be blown, however, I have found some Flutes on which I cou'd blow if after the following manner but you must not expect to find it Indifferently on all Flutes, 'tis play'd by stoping at once the 1st, 2nd and 4th and half the 5th and opening the 3rd, 6th and 7th and blowing very Sharp; Yet I have not inserted it in my Scale by reason 'tis not a Note on which we may depend'.

Ex.94

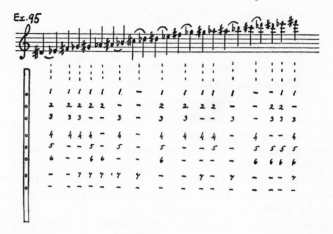

Ex.95

Note that one fingering has to serve for certain enharmonics, D-sharp/E-flat and A-sharp/B-flat in the bottom octave, C-sharp/D-flat and D-sharp/E-flat in the middle register, F-sharp/G-flat, A-sharp/B-flat and C-sharp/D-flat in the upper octave but that distinctions are made between F-sharp and G-flat in the lower octave, G-sharp and A-flat and D-sharp/E-flat in the upper octave. You will see that there is no top F.

Richard Shepherd Rockstro, in his book on the flute first published by Rudall, Carte and Co. in 1890, gives a 'Table of the Fingering of the One-Keyed Flute' by Louis Hotteterre dated 1699. This, also, omits the high F but differs from the English system in that he gives one fingering for the low G-sharp/A-flat, separate fingerings for the F-sharp/G-flat (top line and space of the treble stave), one fingering for the G-sharp/A-flat (next door), separate again for the top C-sharp/D-flat and one for the top D-sharp/E-flat.

The 'traversiere' of Concerto No. 5, is, as noted previously, the normal cross flute. Bach requires the following notes from it, i.e. a smaller compass than he demands from the recorder but chromatic throughout:

Ex.96.

G

ANALYSIS:

CONCERTO NO. 5 IN D MAJOR

Une Traversiere, ⎫
Une Violino principale, ⎬ Concertante
⎭

Une Violino è una Viola in Ripieno

Violoncello, Violone è

Cembalo Concertato

In this work we return to the more normal concerto grosso layout consisting of a concertante group, a ripieno and a continuo.

Bach does not make his intentions perfectly plain in his title but we know full well what he means. His wishes would have been clearer if he had put the 'Cembalo concertato' in the first group; left the words 'in ripieno' until after 'Violoncello' and put 'Violone' with 'Basso Continuo', then the title would have read:

Une Traversiere,

Une Violino principale è Cembalo

Concertato,

Une Violino, una Viola è

Violoncello in Ripieno,

Violone è Cembalo Continuo.

Later copies of the score were more explicit, e.g. one copy in the Berlin Library refers to the work as 'Concerto per il Cembalo Del Sigr. G. S. Bach' and under this title is written: 'Il Clavicembalo, Il Flauto, il Violino ed il Violoncello sono obbligati è soli, l'altre parti sono ripieno'. This agrees with other copies of the score in regarding the cello as one of the solo instruments.

Spitta, Volume 2, page 134, says of Concerto No. 5: 'It is not a strict clavier concerto with accompaniment but the clavier combines with the violin and flute to form a contrasting group with the tutti: in this a second harpsichord for accompanying only was probably introduced, in accordance with Bach's usual practice, even in concertos for the clavier only'. . . . 'Before the last tutti there is a great clavier solo which demands, as does also the other clavier part, a finger dexterity which no one except Bach could have possessed at that time'.

Perhaps Bach intended the cembalo player to combine the functions of concertato and continuo. The part is written out in full for the solo and soli passages and figured and marked 'accompagnamento' in the purely continuo sections. There is, however, something to be gained by having two harpsichords and two players, one solo and one continuo, as Spitta suggests.

The Bach Reader mentions that 'In ensemble music Bach changed the role of the harpsichord in instrumental combinations from that of mere accompanying instrument to that of full partner. The harpsichord, furthermore had never been made the soloist in a concerto. Bach wrote and arranged concertos not only for one harpsichord but also for two, three and four with accompanying instruments'.

Note that the composer asks for first violins only in the orchestra. This does not mean that the conductors should switch all the second violins over to play with the firsts. The Lord forbid that a solo flute, solo violin, and solo harpsichord should be accompanied by about fourteen first and twelve second violins all playing the same line! Bach's normal two or three violins, one or two violas and one cello, plus, of course, violone and continuo harpsichord, provide all the background required. We are told by C. P. E. Bach that Johann Sebastian liked to play viola in the orchestra when possible but took over the solo harpsichord part in this work himself leaving the viola part to be played by the second violinist— hence no music written for the second violins.

First Movement (Allegro).

This movement opens with an eight-bar tutti in which the solo violin joins forces with the ripieno but the flute and solo harpsichord are silent.

Notice particularly A (bar 1), B (bars 3 and 6) and C (bars 7 and 8) given in this extract. Great use is made of these phrases throughout the movement:

The soloists enter at bar 9. Their thematic material consists of:

(i) a falling phrase of four notes discussed between flute and violin and which produces thirds, sixths and tenths with a similar but ornamented phrase in the harpsichord:

(ii) an upward-rising phrase in triplets which often comes in conjunction with (i):

(iii) a phrase, in quavers, based on B:

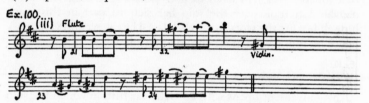

(iv) an extended semiquaver figure based on C:

Notice the rising triplet phrase (ii) (Ex. 99) being shared between the flute and violin and the tenths between the two staves of the harpsichord commencing at bar 16.

There is a neat little conversation between (a) solo violin and viola and (b) flute and viola in bars ten and thirteen; it is a nice difference of opinion as to whether the semiquavers should rise or descend.

The material in the opening half-bar comes in quite useful during the course of the movement, see, for example, bars 35, 36 and 37, the arpeggio accompaniment provided by violin, viola and cello.

Bar 47 introduces the first of the solo harpsichord's cadenza passages consisting of three bars of demi-semiquaver scales which appear again in bar 139. This is the beginning of the great cadenza, it is accompanied for fifteen bars and then goes on as an absolute solo for a further sixty-five bars.

The writing of the fair copy gave Bach an opportunity of revising this cadenza. In an earlier version it is of nineteen bars only. Bach inserts new material between bars 153 and 155 of this early version so that its bar 155 becomes bar 198 in Brandenburg's copy. There are also further changes and additions later on in the cadenza.

Two new figures appear in bar 71. The first (D), an imitative passage shared between flute and violin, extends for ten bars. The second (E), consists of broken-chord semiquavers in the harpsichord which run on for thirty bars:

Flute and violin introduce a broken-chord or arpeggio figure at the eleventh bar of this harpsichord figure (bar 81 of the movement). (Stems of the flute's notes are written upwards—those of the violin pointing downwards):

It provides a most effective accompaniment in conjunction with quaver thirds in the upper strings alternating with an arpeggio on the cello and extends for twelve bars. Later, at bar 95, these two accompanimental figures combine.

Bar 110 brings us back to the music which appeared in bar 9 immediately after the opening tutti and goes on much as before until bar 139. In bar 147 the arpeggio figure (Ex. 104), reappears but with two notes per instrument instead of the former three.

The movement closes with a repetition of the opening tutti.

Second Movement (Affetuoso).

This movement, in B minor, is written for flute, violin and harpsichord only, but I see no objection to the violone doubling the bass of the harpsichord in the purely accompanimental passages. The addition of the stringed instrument helps to point the division between the solo and ripieno sections.

It is of interest that in this concerto the second movement is devoted entirely to the solo instruments. In Concerto No. 3 *all* the players are soloists but here there is a definite soli group separated from the ripieno and it is for this group that Bach writes his slow movement. He went to great pains to work this movement out in detail and did not write merely two cadential chords as in No. 3. I feel this suggests that not more than one solo instrument is intended to provide the slow movement in that particular work. If I am correct in my supposition then obviously the harpsichord is indicated—one unaccompanied solo violin would sound far too small and thin between the quite massive string writing of the outer movements.

The movement is based on two themes, the first with three variants, the second with two. Taking the first group, we hear, in order, A, Ai and Aii:

Ex. 105.

It will be noted that Aii continues up the scale for an octave while Ai drops back a seventh in bar 2. It might, perhaps, be suggested that this was done to avoid carrying the line too high but as this does not apply in bar 21 we must conclude that Bach intended to give a slightly different shape to the theme.

The first version, B, of the second group appears first in the right hand of the harpsichord at bar 7:

Ex. 106.

The variant, Bi, is the semiquaver part of the theme inverted, thus:

Ex. 107

This also makes its first appearance in the right hand of the harpsichord.

The A group returns in part in bar 18 and in full in bars 21 onwards, this time in the key of F minor.

Bach makes considerable use of these semiquaver figures during the course of the movement; see, for example, bars 26–29—also a similar phrase in sixths in bars 40 and 41.

A canon between flute and violin is introduced in bars 30 and 31. Note that the composer has to change the final note of each group of four semiquavers in the violin part.

Bi returns in bar 34 and the A group, complete, is used to terminate the movement in bars 45–49.

Third Movement (*Allegro*).

This, the last movement, is a Jig in ⁶⁄₈ time and is full of mock-fugal entries. Notice that Bach makes use of the conventional writing of

Ex. 108

the period, i.e. his written 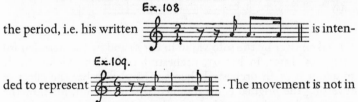 is inten-

Ex. 109.

ded to represent . The movement is not in

a mixture of ²⁄₄ and ⁶⁄₈ but is in ⁶⁄₈ throughout. It opens with the main Theme, A, on the violin followed by the flute. Almost the whole of the passage is then repeated by the harpsichord but with a different ending to make up for the two bars cut out, as it were, between 13 and 14:

Ex. 110.

In bar 19 the harpsichord introduces a pleasantly rippling passage in thirds—B:

Ex. 111.

This re-appears on the same instrument in bars 52–58; 68–75 (in tenths); in an extended form in 110–121; again in 176–193 (slightly varied this time); in 247–253 and, finally, in 280–285.

Flute and violin enjoy some of the customary dovetailing passages from bar 25.

Commencing at bar 35 the orchestra and soloists indulge in imitation derived from bars 5–8 of the opening. The orchestral violins, here (bars 44 and 45) tutti and, later (bars 89–96 and 99–106), one solo player, join the soloists to complete group harmony or to take over a melodic strand from a soloist.

In bar 79 the flute launches a new theme (C) based on bar 1 of the opening phrase:

Ex. 112.

It is taken over by the solo violin in bar 89 and by the harpsichord in bar 99. Later, in bar 148, orchestral violins and violas decide to adopt it as an orchestral theme. This device has the effect of reversing the original concertante v. ripieno layout, for now the upper orchestral strings become the concertante and the three soloists combine to provide the ripieno accompaniment. The theme is accompanied at first (bar 79) (Ex. 112), by solo violin and harpsichord but when the solo violin plays it (bar 89), flute and one solo (orchestral) violin with harpsichord provide the three-stranded accompaniment. Again, when, in bar 99, the harpsichord has the melody, the two solo instruments plus one orchestral violin join together as accompaniment.

On page 23 I quoted Carl Dolmetsch as saying that he believed Bach intended all parts, both soli and ripieno, to be played by single players. But—and it is a big 'but'—in bar 88 (see, if possible, the facsimile edition) Bach writes these words in the first orchestral violin part: 'pianissimo solo'. Eight bars later (bar 96) he writes 'forte' and two bars later again (bar 98) 'pianissimo solo'. There is no 'tutti' mark to counteract the 'solo' but in bar 106 Bach writes 'f' and, as the style of the writing reverts to the purely orchestral from here, one can, I think, assume that this bar, as also does bar 96, marks the beginning of a tutti passage.

There are also (bars 157–8; 161–2; 181–2) tutti statements of the first portion of the theme. This interjection of a few notes of a theme or, maybe, the first bar or so of a tutti is so characteristic of the composer as almost to constitute a trade mark or thumbprint.

A passage shared between flute and solo violin, commencing at bar 193, opens with a rising fourth as though it is going to be yet another statement of the main theme but changes its mind and turns into a little piece of imitation. This is followed (bar 199) by one of Bach's favourite sequential progressions.

At bar 220 a succession of entries of the main subject, A (Ex. 110) leads, via a flourish in tenths on the harpsichord, to a full-close in B minor. A D-major chord in the next bar, however, launches a da capo of the first seventy-eight bars of the movement.

CHAPTER VI

BRANDENBURG CONCERTO
No. 6 in B flat major
à

due Viole da Braccio,
due Viole da Gamba,
Violoncello,
Violone a Cembalo.

This work introduces certainly one new instrument—the viola da gamba—and, perhaps, a second—the viola da braccio. Let us consider the former first.

VIOLA DA GAMBA

The viola da gamba stands in the same relationship to the viols as does the cello to the present-day violins, i.e. it is the baritone voice.

The two family groups may be set out thus:

Viols	Violins
Descant or treble viol	Violin
Alto or tenor viol	Viola
Viola da Gamba	Cello
Violone	Contrabass.

The viola da gamba or 'leg-viol' was so called to distinguish it from the viola da braccio or 'arm-viol'. It was held between the player's legs—as is the modern cello—but did not rest on a spike or peg. The viola, on the other hand, is held 'on the arm' in the same way as a violin and not rested on the knee in a manner similar to an alto viol.

The gamba was a six-stringed instrument until about 1685 (the year of Bach's birth) when a lower (seventh) string was added. The

Ex. 113.

lowest string of the six-stringed gamba was tuned to

Ex. 114

and the seventh string took the compass down to

8va -----

It seems, however, that Bach preferred the six-stringed variety for only twice does he write for the seven, and on only three occasions does he ask his player to tune his low D string down to C.

The range required from the instrument in Concerto No. 6 is

from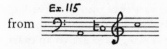

The instrument, which had gut frets similar to the modern guitar, was lightly strung so that its tone was not as full as the cello and it was more reedy in character. Those who have heard the wonderful gamba obbligato in the St Matthew Passion really well played will know its capabilities and lovely tone colour.

There has been a certain amount of discussion in recent years as to whether or not gambas should be fretted for present-day use. August Wenzinger, the famous director of the Scholar Cantorum Basiliensis, discussed this point with me recently and I quote from one of his letters: 'I always play with frets, because not only do they add to the beauty of the real colour of the viol, it is as well historically the right manner. Marin Marais, the great French player of his time, wrote his viol-music with very complicated double-stop technique, which absolutely demands the frets if it is to be played 'Virtuoso'. You will perhaps also have noticed that on old paintings the frets are never missing. I am quite sure that the big artists of their time did not keep the frets because they needed them to find the notes but because the manner of playing and the silvery, floating music caused thus, gave the most satisfying results'.

Certainly in this letter Wenzinger refers to the 'viol' and 'viol-music' but the gamba is, after all, a bass-viol and my inquiry to him was specifically on the fretting, or otherwise, of the gamba.

There was, however, one case in particular, in which I would have thought fretting to be very necessary. It was the custom for most gentlemen to keep chests of viols, i.e. cases containing from four to six instruments of varying sizes. Callers were expected to be capable of taking on a part in a Fantasia or In Nomine on any one of the viols at sight. String players will know how off-putting it is to change from one sized instrument to another several times during the course of an evening and in this case frets would enable the player to have some control over his intonation.

Playford, in his *A Brief Introduction To the Skill of Musick for Song and Viol*.

In Two Books. (First Book for Voice). Second Book, Directions for the Playing on the Viol de Gamba, and also on the Treble-Violin, published in 1658, says (on page 66 and onwards):

(Gamba) 'Belonging to these six strings there are Seven Frets or Stops, which are for stopping or giving variety of Sounds, according to the several Notes of the Gamut on your Instrument, both Flats and Sharps. I have therefore in the following Page drawn an exact Table of the several Notes of the Gamut, in their places, as they are stopt on the several Frets of the Bass Viol, on every string distinctly, beginning with your sixth string, which expresses the lowest Note, and so ascending the several Notes of Scale or Gamut, both Flats and Sharps, till you come to the highest Note usual on the Treble string'.

(page 72) 'These directions for the Bass Viol will also serve for the Treble Viol, which is strung with six strings in the same manner, but is Tuned eight Notes higher, a G. sol re ut on the Treble is an Eight above G. sol re ut on the Bass, and is stopped on the same Fret that it is on the Basse, and so the other Notes according.'

(page 79) Instructions for the Treble Violin: '. . . but before I set down the manner of the Tuning, you must take this Rule, the which though it be not Usual, yet it is very necessary for Young beginners to have their Violin Fretted with six Frets or Stops on the Neck thereof, and that for two reasons, First he shall with more ease find the right stop of every Note; Second, he shall thereby with more ease stop every Note in Tune, which some beginners who learn without, can never attain so good an Ear to stop all Notes in their exact Tune, therefore you must procure your Violin to be Exactly Fretted by a skilful hand to the true distances of half and whole Notes, which done, this following Table (which is drawn according to the Neck of the Treble Violin with four strings and six frets) it being rightly understood, will direct to stop every Note either Flat or Sharp, in his right place; and also to Tune your Violin according to Rules of the Gamut.'

Note that when speaking of the Gamba he says: 'Belonging' to these . . . strings there are . . . Frets' whereas later on he says of the Violin: '. . . you must procure your Violin to be Exactly Fretted. . .' thereby implying that it was not normal for the Violin to be fretted but very useful to a beginner. In fact, they do not 'belong' to this instrument as they do to the Gamba.

VIOLA DA BRACCIO

Now we may return to the viola da braccio.

In the concertos Nos. 1–5 Bach asks for 'Viola' (No. 1); 'Viola' (No. 2); 'Tre viole' (No. 3); 'Una Viola' (No. 4); 'Una Viola' (No. 5); but 'due Viole da Braccio' in No. 6.

Praetorius. in his *Tabella Universalis* gives names and string tunings of some members of the violin family and includes the following:

(No. 3) 'Tenor-Geig' (i.e. the modern viola tuning). Terry states (*Bach's Orchestra'*, page 121): 'The two viole da braccio Bach uses in the sixth Brandenburg concerto

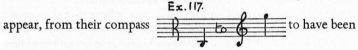

appear, from their compass to have been the alto (No. 3) rather than the true tenor (No. 4) " 'Bass-Geig de

Braccio" '

A 'bass-geig de braccio' of the pitch given would be an uncomfortable handful to hold under the chin. In 1936 I visited Mittenwald and talked to a fiddle maker there who had made several copies of what he called 'a Bach barytone'. It was tuned a tone higher than Praetorius' example No. 4 and was, therefore, an octave below the violin. The models I tried had beautifully warm, soft, tone. I could just manage them under the chin but the maker told me he was sure they should be played cello-wise.

The viola player in a Viennese Chamber group which visited London in May, 1959, used an instrument carrying four playing strings tuned as a viola and, in addition, four sympathetic strings. It was, therefore, a cross between the normal viola and a viola d'amore. This type of instrument was known and used from about 1700 onwards and could, perhaps, have been what Bach had in mind for his concerto. Its shape was, roughly, so:

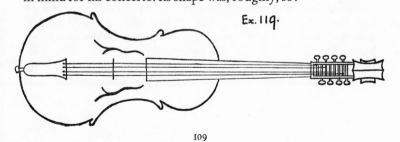

Ex. 119.

One would not expect to find Concerto No. 6—written in or before 1718—in a collection of six concerti as it is really no more a concerto than is the so-called 'Italian' for harpsichord. It is 'concerted' in the sense that it is written for a group of players performing together, apart from that, it is, I feel, pure chamber music but, as in contemporary concerti grossi, the instruments are divided into two groups. The larger consists of two violas, two gambas and a cello and the smaller a violone and a keyboard instrument. Ideally this should be a harpsichord for the first and last movements and a chamber organ for the slow movement.

Bach writes for his gambas in the tenor clef throughout this work but I have put my examples into either the alto or bass clef—whichever seemed more convenient at the moment.

The viola parts are difficult and I do not believe that they could have been played by Leopold's usual violists other than Bach himself. One can daydream a little and eavesdrop on an imaginary conversation between Bach and Leopold's principal violin after rehearsal one morning. 'Dear Herr Bach' (or however he was addressed), 'our other viola player does make a horribly scratchy noise. You yourself have proved to our master the Prince that the viola is, after all, a musical instrument, so would you consider writing a work with no violin parts and giving the top line to the violas? Perhaps you and I could play it? As you know, I am a pretty good fiddler and I also play the viola very well. I'm sure that together we would produce a nicer sound than those terrible cooks and coachmen on our back desks!'

This is, perhaps, a somewhat fanciful explanation but one is forced to wonder at certain aspects of Bach's writing in this work, and, possibly, reassess the date of its composition.

Assuming that Bach intended to play the first viola line himself, then whoever played the second line, whether he was one of the regular viola players or, much more probably, one of the violinists (perhaps Speiss or Markus), must have been possessed of equal technical facility. There is nothing to choose between the two lines from the point of view of difficulty.

Similar considerations apply to the gamba players. The composer had Abel (renowned as a gambist) and, possibly, Leopold himself who was known to play the gamba in addition to the violin and harpsichord, and Linigke—a good cellist—on the cello line. Obviously Bach had a high opinion of Abel for did he not write the three gamba/harpsichord sonatas and the cello suites for him?

Why, then, did he give the gambas only simplified versions of, for example, the cello's theme (B) (in bar 17) when they entered at bars 18 and 19? Why did he cut both gambas out of the slow movement completely and why give them such a very minor role to play in the last movement?

It has become fashionable to assign the composition of this work to the year 1718, i.e. to Bach's second year at Cöthen. Could it be, however, that this assessment is wrong and that it dates back to, say, 1716 when Bach was at Weimar and, therefore, unable to call upon, or be assured of, the services of, such a fine player as Abel? Another possibility concerning the second and third movements is that Bach had written only the first movement when he went to Berlin in 1718 and so was able to show Brandenburg that movement only and to give him an idea of what he had in mind for the remainder of the work. Perhaps Brandenburg had no gamba players in his orchestra at that time (remembering, of course, that Emmerling, who played harpsichord and gamba, was in Brandenburg's service in 1734) and reminded Bach that there was no point in writing a work which included instruments not readily available.

ANALYSIS

First Movement.

The melodic interest in the opening is allotted to the two violas which play the theme, A, (Ex. 120), in canon at a distance of a quaver for fifteen bars. The fact that the second viola's notes are identical with the first's is not quite apparent, especially in certain bars, e.g. 2, 7, 9, etc, until one sees them written out with exactly similar note groupings which, in the case of the second viola, go across the bar lines:

Ex. 120.

III

The lower strings keep up a steady repeated quaver accompaniment throughout this section.

These lower-pitched instruments come to the fore in the seventeenth bar and the cello introduces a canonic theme, B, (Ex. 121), very much in keeping with what has gone before:

This is taken up by the violas while the two gambas present a simplified version. The cello stops after announcing the theme but the violas continue for a few bars with a canon at one bar's distance.

In bar 21 the 1st viola introduces a phrase, C, (Ex. 122) which, repeated a seventh lower at a half-bar's distance by the 2nd viola may, perhaps, be described as 'canonically sequential'—(notes written in treble clef to avoid leger-lines):

At the same time the gambas make great play with the first few notes of A. They give an impression of being about to launch a most significant theme but it does not develop. I have, however, labelled their little phrase as D (Ex.123):

At bar 26 A returns again in the violas and in the key of F but for only two bars and bar 28 brings back the B group with the 1st viola in the lead being followed by cello and the 2nd viola. Then an imitative passage based on the semiquaver figure in B, again divided between violas and cello, appears in bar 30. This is followed by the B group once more led, as at first, by the cello.

Bar 36 ushers in C with its accompaniment D (Ex. 122 and 123), and, in bars 40 and 41, the 1st viola has a little solo passage, but after this has been repeated three times in six bars the 2nd viola restates the main theme (A). After six bars the 1st viola plays the solo twice more. Then, in bar 56, the cello brings back the B phrase again.

The C and D groups return in bar 62 and the main theme A at bar 73. In bar 84 the 1st viola is allowed one statement of the solo after which the 2nd viola resumes the A theme and leads the canon, leaving the 1st viola to follow a quaver later. However, the 1st viola resorts to a little rhythmic trick in bar 89 and so manages to lead the canon by a quaver once more.

The bars 40/41 passage—partially in canon at the half-bar—between the two violas is introduced again in bar 92 and accompanied by a nearly similar passage on the 1st gamba. Later, bar 96, the 2nd viola leads in the C and D phrases.

In bar 101 the two violas and the 1st gamba introduce an attractive three-part round. This is not allowed to go on for long, however, for half-way through bar 102 the cello brings back B with its attendant phrases on the two gambas and the violas. This leads on to C with D (bar 107) and the main A theme returns half-way through bar 114. The music continues, as in the opening of the work but two beats later, in bar position right through to the end of the movement; the final chord coming on the third beat instead of the first as in the corresponding cadence in bar 17.

Second Movement (Adagio ma non tanto).

One would expect this movement to be in either F major—the dominant of B-flat, or G-minor—the relative minor of B-flat, whereas, in fact, it opens in E-flat major (keeping, of course, its two-flat key signature). The key reverts to B-flat in bar 8 and the cadence is repeated three bars later.

Note that the gambas are silent throughout this movement and, with the exception of a three-bar cadenza in bars 54 to 56 for the cello and two bars of counterpoint in bars 59 and 60 together with two false entries and one four-bar attempt at the opening theme for the same instrument (bars 40, 42 and 44-47), the movement is a duet for the two violas.

The melodic material consists of nine statements of a theme of which the first three bars are similar in each statement but which are varied later:

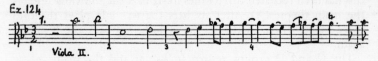

Ex. 124

1. (2nd viola) commencing in bar 1.
2. (1st viola) commencing in bar 4.
3. (2nd viola) commencing in bar 11.
4. (1st viola) commencing in bar 14 and similar to No. 2.
5. (1st viola) commencing in bar 20 similar to No. 1 for four bars and then changing into No. 3.
6. (2nd viola) commencing in bar 24 and similar to No. 2.
7. (2nd viola) commencing in bar 30 and similar to No. 5.
8. (1st viola) commencing in bar 34 and similar to No. 2.
9. (1st viola) commencing in bar 48 and similar to No. 2.

There is a false entry, i.e., the theme minus the first two bars, from the 2nd viola at bar 40, this is repeated by the 1st viola and again by the 2nd in consecutive bars and yet again by the 2nd viola in bar 44, at the same time as the cello entries are attempted.

There is a suggestion of a 10th statement of the theme in bar 54 from both violas in which the first two notes are made three times their former length, i.e. the two minims become dotted semibreves and the third note is lengthened to seven crochet beats instead of four.

The music is, quite unmistakably, in G minor by bars 58 and 59 and closes on a chord of D major (the dominant of the relative minor), in bar 62. This D major chord serves to swing the work back into its home key, B-flat, for the last movement—a $\frac{12}{8}$ Jig.

Third Movement (Allegro).

The violas are in unison for the first eight bars in which they announce the main theme, A:

Ex. 125.

The syncopations of the 3rd, 5th and 7th bars are quite a feature of the movement.

The two gambas return to the score in this movement but in a very minor capacity. All they have to do is to fill-in or complete some viola or cello harmony. The cello, on the other hand, is given material of considerable interest and importance and has several semiquaver passages.

At the end of the 8th bar both violas seem to wish to introduce a new theme, B. I say 'seem to wish' advisedly as they each have two attempts before succeeding at the third. Even then there is disagreement as the 1st viola returns to the syncopations of bar 3 of A and leaves the 2nd viola to develop the semiquaver figures of B:

Ex.126.

After three bars of this quite friendly disagreement they unite with two bars of A and then decide to return to B in the key of F and with the 2nd viola leading. Again, after three bars, both violas concentrate on the syncopations in A and then the 2nd viola, followed by the 1st, reverts to the semiquaver figures as accompaniment or counterpoint (see bars 20 and 21, etc. and call this phrase 'C').

In bar 23, violas introduce a new effect, an imitative passage, D (Ex. 127). The 2nd viola ruins the first attempt by breaking off into semiquavers. However, the second try nearly comes off and the third is successful:

Ex.127.
D.

H*

This is followed by one bar of A (which seems to serve as a rallying point) then C (in bar 28), part of B (bar 32), again a bar of A (Bar 34), then a few bars of C and so back to A complete (bars 38–45).

Let us return to the early part of the movement to examine the cello line. It contains a smooth quaver passage at bar 9 and again at bar 15. While the violas are experimenting with D in bars 23 and onwards (Ex. 127), Bach introduces a semiquaver figure akin to the second part of the violas' B into the cello part. It doesn't get very far with its first attempt before breaking off into quavers but the second try, after an initial false start, nearly succeeds, for after a couple of bars the cellist feels able to ask the world to listen to *him* for a change (bar 27 and onwards)! One is tempted to think that Bach wrote quite a lot of this work, especially the last movement, with his tongue firmly in his cheek, for it abounds with touches of humour. In the midst of their experiments with B around bars 29 and 30 the violas appear to listen to the cello's quavers. It proves fatal! First the 2nd viola forgets to play leaving the 1st on his own: then No. 1 stops and the 2nd has to rush in in order to keep the ball rolling after which they both pull themselves together again for long enough to reach phrase B at bar 32.

At the end of bar 45 the 1st viola announces a short cadenza-like, passage. The 2nd viola joins in at the next bar. The effect of this, with the 2nd viola joining in, is, or should be, of a passage of double stopping between octave drones:

Ex. 128.

After two bars together the violas stage an arpeggio playing contest (bars 48 and onwards).

Two bars of the main theme, A, at bars 52–53, lead to a restatement of D in a slightly embellished version. This embellishment really dictates the speed of the movement—which is, of course, a Jig—it must move at a good pace but such ornaments should not sound jumbled, therefore the exact pace of the Allegro is dictated by the 1st viola's technique.

Bar 58 introduces a inverted version of the bar 45 cadenza passage (with the 2nd viola leading) and a slightly altered arpeggio passage;

then follow the last two bars of A and A complete. The B phrase returns in bar 74 and 80 and runs, via B, to D (bar 88) with the 2nd viola leading as at the phrase's first appearance and with the 2nd's original version in place of the 1st's ornaments. Again, in bars 94 and 95, the violas seem to forget to play in order to listen to the cello's semiquavers and the movement closes with a complete re-statement of the A theme, finishing, curiously enough, on the fourth beat of the bar. (This happened, of course, in the opening, but less obviously as then the B phrase followed without a break).

PART III

GRACES—ORNAMENTATION

CHAPTER VII

GRACES—ORNAMENTATION

Eyebrows are raised in horror sometimes at the mere thought of adding an ornament to a Bach work. I cannot understand why. Bach himself would have expected it, for it was customary—and there is no reason at all why his texts should be considered as sacred when other composers of the period, e.g. Handel, are liable to have their texts very freely ornamented.

Obviously the subject is one which requires considerable study, skill and good taste. A dish which is over-relished is as objectionable as one which is too plain, but a dish which the cook serves up unflavoured can be garnished by the eater; similarly, a work which is printed plain can, and should, be graced by the performer—or, better still, the editor.

Bach himself supplies patterns for ornamentation and shows us exactly how we should proceed. An interesting example of the manner in which he ornaments a passage is given by the two versions of the solo violin line in the Andante of Brandenburg Concerto No. 4 in G. In the second version the solo instrument is changed to the keyboard and the whole work transposed down in F. I give the two extracts in parallel.

Ex. 129.

A quite considerable amount of a Bach editor's time needs to be devoted to writing in ornaments and phrases which the composer has left out. Let us examine a few passages of the first movement of Brandenburg Concerto No. 1 in detail. Bar 5 contains this phrase

Ex. 130.

in first oboe and first violin:

The corresponding bar in the Cantata version of the work bears a turn sign between the F and G and in bar 11 of the Concerto the composer provides the clue as to how he wishes such turns to be

Ex. 131.

played by writing the ornament out in full

It seems to me that it is quite legitimate for an editor to add a turn in similar passages.

The first horn launches a most important theme in bar 14 of the same movement and the third quaver of this passage bears a trill

Ex. 132.

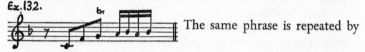

The same phrase is repeated by the horn in bar 59 but without the trill. Surely Bach just forgot to write the sign in or else assumed that, having told the player about the trill once, he would play it automatically in similar passages?

Slurs were classed as ornaments in Bach's day, and he is almost as careless with these as with the more usual forms of decoration. Still considering the first movement of Brandenburg No. 1 we find a slur in the third oboe part in bar 45 and one feels that this phrasing should apply not only to all three oboes but to strings as well—in fact to whichever instruments are concerned with the same or similar passages.

In bar 43 the second oboe (which is in unison with the 2nd violin and in thirds with the 1st oboe and 1st violin) carries a cadential trill on the fourth beat of the bar. The trill sign is not written in any of the other parts—obviously it should be.

One could give hundreds of similar examples from all the works. The constant repetition of the same points would, however, prove very boring to the reader.

Extra ornamentation can and, I feel, should, be added with taste and discretion. The Andante of Concerto No. 2 is a good example of a movement which gains considerably from the inclusion of a few trills such as those added by August Wenzinger in the Scholar Contorum Basiliensis recordings. I would recommend a close study of his performing edition.

One cannot stress too often that in performance the smallest possible number of players should be used, viz:

No. 1

  2 horns
  3 oboes
  1 bassoon
  1 solo violin (piccolo)
  3 1st violins or 1
  3 2nd violins or 1
  2 violas „ or 1
  1 cello
  1 violone or bass
  1 harpsichord
  18 players   or 13

No. 3

  3 violins
  3 violas
  3 celli
  1 bass
  1 harpsichord
  11 players

No. 5

  1 flute
  1 solo violin
  3 violins   or 2
  2 violas   or 1
  1 cello
  1 bass
  1 or 2 harpsichords
  10 or 11 players   or 8 or 9

No. 2

  1 trumpet
  1 recorder
  1 oboe
  1 solo violin
  3 1st violins   or 1
  3 2nd violins   or 1
  2 violas „   or 1
  1 cello
  1 bass
  1 harpsichord
  15 players   or 10

No. 4

  1 solo violin
  2 recorders
  3 1st violins   or 1
  3 2nd violins   or 1
  2 violas   or 1
  1 cello
  1 bass
  1 harpsichord
  14 players   or 9

No. 6

  2 violas
  2 gambas
  1 cello
  1 bass
  1 harpsichord
  doubling chamber
  organ
  7 players

Only in this way will the part be balanced and the works shine with all their perfect clarity and sparkle.

Such performances as we have heard in the Albert Hall of, e.g. No. 3 with: 12 violins to each part

3 or 4 violas to each line

2 or 3 celli to each line

and 8 or so basses with no harpsichord and no slow movement, also (as in pre-war days in the Queen's Hall) No. 6 with 12 violas to a part and four celli playing each gamba line, cannot be condemned strongly enough. It is impossible to think of anything more unlike Bach. To my mind it is just as wrong, stylistically, to 'blow-up' a Bach orchestration as to play a string quartet by Haydn with twelve or so players to each violin part 'balanced' by ten violas and eight celli.

Although these works are written in the style of solo concertos or concerti grossi and for 'Someone's' Court orchestra they are, nevertheless, chamber music in that they were intended to be performed in that 'Someone's' music room and not in a public concert hall. They can, of course, be played quite successfully in the Royal Festival Hall in London with their original instrumentation, because experience has proved that that particular hall is good acoustically for such music but I doubt the wisdom of trying to perform them in London's Royal Albert Hall.

CONCLUSION

I have tried to write about these wonderful works in not too serious a manner. This does not mean that I regard them or their composer lightly, quite the reverse in fact, for I consider them to contain some of the finest music ever written. It does seem advisable, however, to get away as far as possible from the very flowery and long-winded pomposity of writers on music during the last one hundred or so years.

John Playford, in the Preface to his *Introduction to the Skill of Musick* (11th edition, published 1687) says:

'. . . for that the Prescription of Rules of all Arts and Sciences ought to be deliver'd in plain and brief language, and not in Flowers of Eloquence . . .'

Could one ask for better advice?

124

INDEX

INDEX I—General

125

INDEX II—Names & Places

INDEX III—Instruments

Alto-geig 109
alto trombone 45
arm-viol 106

Bach-barytone 109
Bach-trumpet 64
bass(es) 55, 56, 68, 69, 70, 71, 74, 81, 82, 92, 122, 123, 124
bass-gamba 39, 69
Bass-Geig de Braccio 109
bass string 23, 93
bass trombone 45
bass viol 108
basso 39, 40, 41, 68, 75, 84
bassono 41
bassoon 9, 13, 22, 25, 27, 28, 29, 30, 37, 40, 41, 42, 55, 60, 64, 82, 123
blockflöte 67

'cello 9, 23, 26, 27, 28, 29, 30, 39, 40, 41, 55, 68, 69, 71, 75, 76, 77, 78, 79, 80, 81, 82, 87, 92, 93, 99, 101, 106, 107, 110, 111, 112, 113, 114, 115, 116, 117, 123, 124
Cembalo 68, 75, 84, 98
chamber organ 110, 123
clarinet (E-flat) 62
clarino 45, 61, 62, 63, 64
clavicembalo 84, 98
clavier 23, 98
contrabass(o) 40, 41, 84, 106
corno(i) (da caccia) 22, 42, 45, 48, 49, 54, 55, 65

discant trombone 45
double-bass 39, 41

fag (otto) 26
fiauto 67
Fiauti d'Echo 67
fiddle 41
flageolets (bird) 87
flauti d'Echo 83, 84, 86, 90
Flauto (d'eco, dolce, traverso) 67, 68, 69, 83, 84, 98
Flöte 67, 83
flute 9, 14, 25, 26, 27, 28, 29, 30, 45, 67, 81, 86, 94, 96, 97, 98, 99, 100, 101, 102, 103, 104, 105, 123

Flûte (à bec, allemande, d'Allemagne, douce) 67, 83, 86
Flüte traversière 67

gamba, viola da 9, 14, 21, 25, 26, 27, 28, 29, 30, 39, 40, 81, 107, 108, 110, 111, 112, 113, 115, 123, 124
gross quint-bass 40
guitar 107

harpsichord 9, 21, 23, 25, 28, 29, 30, 41, 69, 71, 77, 78, 82, 93, 99, 100, 101, 102, 103, 104, 105, 110, 111, 123, 124
Hautbois 41, 68
Hautboy 36, 37
horns 9, 21, 22, 28, 30, 31, 35, 43, 44, 45, 46, 47, 48, 49, 50, 52, 53, 54, 55, 57, 58, 59, 60, 61, 65, 122, 123
horns (in alt) 43, 44, 45, 46, 51, 52, 65
hunting horn 50, 51

Jagdhorn 13, 22, 31, 64

keyboard 20, 24, 29, 78, 82, 110, 121

large violone 40
leg-viol 106

oboes 9, 13, 22, 26, 27, 28, 29, 30, 35, 36, 37, 38, 45, 46, 48, 49, 53, 54, 55, 56, 57, 58, 60, 68, 69, 70, 71, 72, 73, 74, 122, 123
organ 22, 40, 78

piano 41
piccolo horn 45
post horn 48, 66
principale 61, 62

Querflöte 67

Recorder 9, 13, 28, 30, 48, 67, 68, 70, 71, 72, 73, 74, 83, 85, 86, 87, 88, 89, 90, 91, 92, 123
Recorder (treble) 67, 87
Recorder (sopranino) 87

saxophone (sopranino) 62

129

GEORGE ALLEN & UNWIN LTD
London: 40 Museum Street, W.C.1

Auckland: 24 Wyndham Street
Bombay: 15 Graham Road, Ballard Estate, Bombay 1
Bridgetown: P.O. Box 222
Buenos Aires: Escritorio 454-459, Florida 165
Calcutta: 17 Chittaranjan Avenue, Calcutta 13
Cape Town: 109 Long Street
Hong Kong: 44 Mody Road, Kowloon
Ibadan: P.O. Box 62
Karachi: Karachi Chambers, McLeod Road
Madras: Mohan Mansions, 38c Mount Road, Madras 6
Mexico: Villalongin 32-10, Piso, Mexico 5, D.F.
Nairobi: P.O. Box 4536
New Delhi: 13-14 Asaf Ali Road, New Delhi 1
São Paulo: Avenida 9 De Julho 1138-Ap. 51
Singapore: 36c Prinsep Street, Singapore 7
Sydney, N.S.W.: Bradbury House, 55 York Street
Tokyo: 10 Kanda-Ogawamachi, 3-Chome, Chiyoda-Ku
Toronto: 91 Wellington Street West, Toronto 1

K. GEIRINGER

THE BACH FAMILY

Through more than two centuries the Bach Family supplied Thuringia with cantors, organists and outstanding composers. This great work is the first complete history of this amazing family from the sixteenth century miller Veit to Wilhelm Friedrich Ernst (1759-1845), Johann Sebastian's grandson.

The author views the family as a whole and shows the characteristic similarities in their artistic and human attitudes as well as the most significant divergences. Equal stress is laid on the discussion of the personalities, against the swiftly changing historical scene, and of the music, for which the author was able to use vast, hitherto inaccessible material. The three main sections of this book describe: the rise of the Bach family and the first great achievements up to 1700; their expansion and culmination (1700-1750); the last great Bach composers and the decline of the family (1750-1845).

Although this is not primarily intended as a new biography of Johann Sebastian, the very extensive section dealing with his life and work presents a wealth of details new to the English reader. Apart from describing the fascinating phenomenon of this musical family the author gives a history of musical thought in the last three hundred years. Illustrations include hitherto unknown portraits of the leading members, and an immense number of musical examples.

Demy 8vo   *50s. net*

BRAHMS
His Life and Work
Demy 8vo   *21s. net*

HAYDN
A Creative Life in Music
Demy 8vo   *21s. net*

MUSICAL INSTRUMENTS
Their History from the Stone Age
to the Present Day
Demy 8vo   *35s. net*

GEORGE ALLEN & UNWIN LTD